The New Bride Guide
by Ellie Kay

Books by Ellie Kay

How to Save Money Every Day

Money Doesn't Grow on Trees

The New Bride Guide

Shop, Save, and Share

THE New Bride GUIDE

ELLIE KAY

BETHANYHOUSE

MINNEAPOLIS, MINNESOTA

Published by Bethany House Publishers
A Ministry of Bethany Fellowship International
11400 Hampshire Avenue South
Bloomington, Minnesota 55438
www.bethanyhouse.com

Printed in the United States of America

Library of Congress Cataloging-in-Publication Data

Kay, Ellie.
    The new bride guide : everything you need to know for the first year of marriage / by Ellie Kay.
        p. cm.
      ISBN 0-7642-2694-0 (pbk.)
      1. Marriage. 2. Home economics. 3. Weddings—Planning. 4. Wives—Life skills guides. I. Title.

HQ734 K352 2003
306.81—dc21   2002151886

This book is dedicated to
Lee and Paula Hough.
May your first year of marriage be rich and full of joy.
Good things come to those who wait.

ELLIE KAY is founder and author of *Shop, Save, and Share* Seminars and a gifted speaker and writer. She is a graduate of Colorado Christian University with a degree in management of human resources. She and her husband, Bob, a Stealth fighter pilot with the U.S. Air Force, have five children, two adult children, and make their home in New Mexico.

Ellie's first book, *Shop, Save, and Share*, presents a streamlined program to help families save hundreds of dollars a month on groceries and household supplies—and have an abundance to share with people in need. Filled with her signature humor and real-life stories, it contains easy-to-apply principles that allow most households to lower their food budgets 50 to 85 percent under national norms.

A wise and witty communicator, Ellie is a regular guest on CNBC's *Power Lunch* and a national radio commentator for *Money Matters*.

If you wish to contact Ellie Kay for speaking engagements or media, she can be reached at:

Ellie Kay
P.O. Box 202
Alamogordo, NM 88311-0202

e-mail: *ellie@elliekay.com*
Web site: *www.elliekay.com*

Acknowledgments

My thanks go to the people who made this book possible, for it takes many people to bring thoughts and ideas to life. Steve Laube first had the idea of a guide for new brides, and I thank him for entrusting me with the vision for this endeavor. Lee Hough is the "World's Greatest Literary Agent" and provided tremendous insight to this project—even as he practices the premises found in this book. Congratulations on your first year of marriage to Paula; your contributions will enrich the lives of those who read and apply the principles found herein. I thank Julie Klassen, who does such great editorial work. Rachel St. John Gilbert was an important set of eyes on this manuscript, and I thank her for all her hard work, honest reflections, and last-minute craziness from a woman under deadline.

I once read a quote by an (anonymous) author that said: "I have been writing all my life, and I've yet to figure out a better method to writing books than to write like crazy for the month before it is due and then spend the next month apologizing to my family." I believe I need to do this as well! Many apologies to my husband, Bob, and the kids: Daniel, Philip, Bethany, Jonathan, Joshua, Missy, and Mandy for the missed dinners, mounds of laundry, and preoccupied expression on my face. You are a fabulous support team, and no amount of praise or accolades would satisfy apart from you all.

The greatest thanks go to God above, who is so faithful to "anoint my pen and redeem my time." I could do nothing worthwhile apart from the Creator of the Universe.

As I read the manuscript for this book, I was amazed at the abundance of helpful and insightful information the author was able to pull together. What a difference this book will make in any woman's life! Questions and concerns of brides are anticipated and answered practically and thoroughly, and many subjects a bride never anticipates until it's too late are also addressed. As you turn each page, you will discover something new and helpful to make your wedding experience and your first year of marriage all you want it to be.

You will welcome this book as the best resource on the market today for helping a bride make her wedding planning easier and more enjoyable. This is a resource that was needed decades ago! You'll find yourself telling others about what you've learned again and again. Don't be surprised if wedding planners and counselors begin looking to you for answers because of your newly acquired wisdom.

H. Norman Wright
Licensed Marriage, Child, and Family Therapist

CONTENTS

The Princess Bride
on a Cinderella Budget

Balancing Wedding and Honeymoon Resources

CHAPTER 1

Shower the One You Love With Love

How to Organize Pre-Wedding Events to Save on Post-Wedding Costs

"This is *the* most romantic movie in the world!" my ten-year-old daughter Bethany sobbed, "Please pass the tissues!"

The movie in the videotape player continued, *Oh, Darling! I'll meet you at the top of the Empire State Building in six short months! I'll be there, dearest, I'll be there.* Then Cary Grant takes Deborah Kerr in his arms and kisses her passionately in that timeless classic *An Affair to Remember.*

I teared up as well, knowing that the heroine was destined to be crippled by a taxicab and would never make that fateful meeting.

Our hothouse of feminine emotions was rudely interrupted by my thirteen-year-old son: "I can't believe this! Why are you sobbing over *that!* It's just a movie, and a pretty lame one at that!"

I immediately banished him to go play basketball with his three brothers outside. Men! They just never "get" these divine chick flicks!

But Bethany and I did. I blubbered through *Sleepless in Seattle* in the same way—especially when I thought that Meg Ryan would miss Tom Hanks, who was at the top of the Empire State Building on Valentine's Day.

So when I discovered that Bob and I would be in New York City for our oldest daughter's graduation from Columbia University on

Valentine's Day, I insisted that Bob and I do the Empire State Building romantic chick-flick thingy.

When I told Bob that we were going to this romantic icon on that evening, "The World's Greatest Fighter Pilot" just groaned, "Do I *have* to?"

It's not that my husband is unromantic—he's just afraid of open heights. You may scoff, "A pilot who's afraid of heights? You gotta' be kiddin'!"

But I'm not. And he is. So there.

"But how can you fly jets?" most people ask my husband when they hear of his phobia. To which he responds,

"In a jet, I'm in control, and I'm surrounded by a canopy that makes me feel like I'm inside a protective space. I'm never scared in a jet unless someone is firing missiles at me. But in open heights—that's a different story!"

The big day arrived, and I was soooo looking forward to our trip to the top of the infamous building. While we were waiting in line with the other romantics, Bob's palms were sweaty, and he kept asking, "Do I *have* to do this?"

We bought our tickets, walked toward the elevators, and just as we approached them, Bob, right on cue, nervously sputtered, "Uh, I'm going to go to the bathroom, I'll meet you at the top."

You see, part of the romance was that we would go up in separate elevators; then when he saw me at the top, he was supposed to say, "I *knew* you'd be here!" Then we would run into each other's arms, and the onlookers would sigh at our sweet spontaneity.

But things never work out the way they do in the movies.

While I was in the elevator, I met some really nice people, and we got to chatting. My friends say that I make new friends everywhere I go. One time when a friend of mine was meeting me at my plane, three different people came up to me as we disembarked and wished me well. "Who were they?" my girl friend asked curiously.

"Oh, they were just new friends I made on the plane." Well, I found myself doing the same thing in the elevator.

As we stepped onto the 102nd floor, my newfound friends wished me well and I went to the observation deck to wait. New York City is *very* cold in February, and the windchill factor at the top of the Empire State Building makes it seem even colder. But I bundled myself in my coat and gloves and waited by the railing for my true love to arrive.

And I waited. And waited. And waited.

My nose started to run.

I began to think that Bob had wimped out as I wiped my reddening schnoz with a Kleenex. My ears began to get cold, and I was *sure* that this was not the way they did it in the movies.

Just when I was about to give up and go back down the elevator to find the "World's Greatest Flying Chicken," I felt a tap on my shoulder. I turned around to find Bob, shivering in his flight jacket with sweat running down his brow.

Mechanically (and very unromantically, I might add) he took my semi-frozen fingers into his icy palms and with chattering teeth uttered, "Oh. It's you. I knew you'd be here . . . Can we go back down now?"

At that moment my elevator friends approached us and I reluctantly introduced them to Bob.

"Oh, we heard all about you on the elevator. How you fly the Stealth and how you're afraid of heights and how you're doing this for your wife!" They smiled and asked to take our picture.

Bob smiled like a wooden soldier and through slightly gritted teeth responded, "Gee, uh . . . that's great. I'm not surprised she told you all about me . . . but I really need to go . . . NOW!"

Ah, the things we do for love.

If you're reading this book, then you're in the same position that Bob was at the top of the Empire State Building—facing the fear of the unknown. You're conquering the uncertainty of a lifelong commitment to another human being. This can be a fearful and yet wonderful time of life, but if you want it to be just like the movies, then you may be in for a disappointment.

In order to keep your dreams of marital bliss from turning into nightmares, there are a few things that it would be wise to keep in mind as you plan for the wedding, honeymoon, and first year of marriage.

During the planning stages of the wedding ceremony, remember these three main points:

> If you haven't started premarital counseling already, then run, don't walk, to the nearest counselor in your area.

1. You're not only planning for a wedding but, more important, for a marriage.
2. This is a one-day event—don't borrow on your future (or your parents') for just one day.
3. You will remember the "feelings" of the day more than the events.

Premarital Counseling

As the first point indicates, this is more about a marriage than a wedding ceremony. If you haven't started premarital counseling already, then run, don't walk, to the nearest counselor in your area. The sessions are most often offered through a local church, but you may also find a qualified counselor through community services.

For more information on these kinds of services and their value, go to *smartmarriages.com* and *marriagesavers.com*. PREPARE is the name of a highly successful program that helps couples get ready for marriage. A million couples have taken PREPARE since 1980, and there are 50,000 trained counselors in the United States. To learn more, visit the *lifeinnovation.com* Web site. Or to locate a trained PREPARE counselor in your area, fill in the information requested at *www.lifeinnovation.com*. Another option is a program called FOCCUS (Facilitating Open Couple Communication, Understanding, and Study). Both of these programs are excellent tools. The

FOCCUS homepage is: *www.parishdatainc.com/focc/fochm.htm.* Direct mail inquiries or phone calls can be directed to:

> Parish Data System, Inc.
> 14425 No. 19th Ave.
> Phoenix, AZ 85023–6702
> *602–789–0595*

Dr. Robert G. Smith, an experienced premarital counselor and one of the individuals who spearheaded the effort for "Covenant Marriage" certificates in Louisiana says, "I would not recommend anyone utilizing a counselor who does not use some kind of premarital inventory. The tools are too valuable and comprehensive compared to the off-the-cuff evaluations done spontaneously. The difference might be likened to a very fine, compassionate family doctor— who doesn't utilize an EKG when your presenting complaint happens to be heart trouble."

Before you commit to any counselor, make sure that he or she shares the same spiritual worldview and that the following topics will be covered:

- personality profiles
- premarital inventory tools
- finances and budgeting
- communication
- diverse backgrounds and their potential impact
- intimacy
- expectations in marriage
- children
- faith
- in-laws

While this list is not exhaustive, and your counselor may cover more areas, counseling is essential to your future marital health. Consider it preventive relational maintenance.

Wedding Budget: Step One

Who's Paying for What?

An old proverb says, "A wise man counts the cost *before* he builds a tower." One of the main mistakes couples make is in not setting a wedding budget, or expecting their parents to cover expenses beyond their ability to pay. It may be hard to ask some of the following questions, but it will be a *lot* harder to ask them after you've already started the financial ball rolling. NOW is the time to gather all your financial facts.

Here are the questions to have answered before you go looking for a dress or ordering invitations.

What expenses will the bride's parents cover and what is the financial limitation? Some parents may give a lump sum, or they will opt to pay for specific expenses, such as the dress and/or reception. Every family is different and has various financial obligations. Don't *assume* they will (or can) cover those expenses that the bride's parents traditionally take care of—talk to them about it ahead of time. How do you broach this uncomfortable topic? Often a direct approach works best. For example, you might say something like: "Mom and Dad, we're figuring out a budget for our wedding (you know how hard that is!), and it's something you and I haven't talked about before. 'Ted' and I are planning to take care of the majority of the costs, but if you would like to help out in any way, it would help us to know that from the outset. If you aren't able to help out financially, we certainly understand and would welcome your advice on _____ , _____ , and _____ (you fill in the blanks)." If you have parents who are in second marriages, gather this information from all the parents involved, giving each the opportunity to participate, while avoiding the implication of obligation. You want cheerful givers, not ones who will hang it over your head throughout the planning stages (or throughout the rest of your lives).

Traditionally, the bride's parents paid for the majority of the expenses, including all ceremony and reception costs (food, wedding cake, music, photos, flowers), the wedding invitations and related expenses, and the bride's attire and trousseau. But with many couples getting married later in life, when they are likely to be more financially independent, these rules have changed, and many times the bride and groom cover the majority of the expenses themselves. In fact, a good option would be to plan a wedding you and your husband-to-be can afford without any parental assistance. Then if assistance is offered, it will be a pleasant surprise that will allow you to do more than you would be able to do otherwise. Paying for your own wedding also eliminates the need to accommodate every whim of the people who are paying for it.

What expenses will the groom's parents cover? I know of a couple who paid for their son's portion of the wedding and then spent the entire time complaining that they were paying more than the bride's parents. This only adds stress to the event and counters the financial benefit of their contribution. Have both parents read this section. Hopefully it will encourage them to contribute willingly without constantly reminding the young couple of their financial assistance.

Traditionally, the groom's parents were only expected to pay for the rehearsal dinner. The groom himself picked up the costs of the marriage license, the bride's engagement and wedding rings, the bride's bouquet, corsages for the mothers, the boutonnieres, the ceremony officiant's fee, and the honeymoon.

Are there any others who have offered to cover specific expenses? Sometimes grandparents or other relatives will offer to pay for part of the honeymoon or something else as their wedding gift to the couple. While it would be poor form to ask people what they're giving you, it's all right to list those offers that have already been made.

What expenses will the bride and groom cover? Many couples receive no assistance from their families for various reasons, and you may fit into this category. The most common expense incurred by the bride and groom is the honeymoon, and this should be figured into the wedding expenses.

Wedding Budget: Step Two

The Best Advice You'll Ever Get

When it comes to counting the cost of your wedding, the very best advice you can follow is simply this: Do not go into debt for the wedding or honeymoon and do not allow those who love you to do so either. If you spend more than you have on a one-day event, not only are you setting a poor precedent for your marriage, but you are also borrowing on your future or the future of those who love you. An online budgeting tool you might want to review can be found at the *weddingchannel.com* Web site. Just go to *http://wedding.weddingchannel.com/pwp/ww_sell.asp* and link onto the budget guide in the planning section. Another favorite of many new brides is *www.theknot.com.* Simple, easy to follow, and full of great checklists. Pick one and use it!

> Do not go into debt for the wedding or honeymoon and do not allow those who love you to do so either.

Wedding Budget: Step Three

Prioritize

As a couple (not with Mom and Dad, but as a *couple*), prioritize what is most important to you about your wedding and honeymoon. It might be that certain aspects of the wedding event are more important than an expensive honeymoon or vice versa. Remember that the intrinsic value of the big day is measured inwardly rather than outwardly. Thus, the categories are differentiated by *Internal* and *External*. Rank each category independently and then as a couple, with #1 being most important and #10 being least important. You may add those things you value that may not be on this list, but there's enough here to get you started:

Internal	He Said	She Said
Positive Honeymoon Experience	_____	_____
Memories of Ceremony	_____	_____
Spiritual Significance	_____	_____
Pleasing Extended Family	_____	_____
Feelings of Romance	_____	_____
Practicality of Ceremony	_____	_____
Brevity of Ceremony	_____	_____
Minimal Embarrassment	_____	_____
Participation of Family Members	_____	_____
Wedding Vows	_____	_____
Other	_____	_____

External	He Said	She Said
Wedding Dress	_____	_____
Flowers	_____	_____
Photos	_____	_____
Reception	_____	_____
Rehearsal Dinner	_____	_____
Honeymoon Trip	_____	_____
Invitations	_____	_____
Gifts for Attendants	_____	_____
Wedding Cake	_____	_____
Decorations for Church	_____	_____
Other	_____	_____

Wedding Budget: Step Four

What Do You Value?

You may wonder how the internal aspects of the wedding fit under a budget heading. Well, you will spend your money on those things that you value most. If you value the spiritual aspect of the ceremony, you may be content to spend less on flowers and more for live music or a printed program for guests. If you value memories, then you will want to spend more money on quality photography rather than letting Uncle Joe use his new camera to cover the event.

At this point, evaluate the two categories and decide what your priorities will be for the wedding and honeymoon according to the answers each of you gave for the previous exercise.

Add all funds available from Step One, paying special attention to Step Two, and use this figure as the working outline for your wedding/honeymoon budget.

Now decide how much you will spend on each category. You may want to call various places and get their low-to-high prices in order to establish an effective working budget. For example, call your local printer or wedding invitation designer and ask about their price ranges for invitations; call the travel agent and ask what it would cost to fly to Tahiti for a week; call a bridal shop and ask the price range for wedding dresses and tuxedo rentals. I will give specific ways to cut costs in most of these areas later, but right now you are establishing a working budget.

Setting Up a Gift Registry

Now that you have a working budget for your special day, it's time to turn your attention to registering for gifts that will help you set up your new home.

Take Inventory

Inventory the items you—and your fiancé—already have. Perhaps you are combining two households, in which case you will not need all the usual trappings that accompany the initial establishment of a home. Go through each room and decide what you really *need*, first, and then what you *want*, second. There may be some items that you may be willing to wait for if you can't get exactly what you want. These, then, aren't true "needs." For example, if you want to have some cool art and have a specific piece in mind because of your taste, you might list the work. Otherwise, you might prefer to pass on receiving art as a gift because you have a specific decorating theme in mind, and you'd rather wait until you can buy just the right thing rather than settle for something else. Be sure to decide on colors and patterns. Do not include those items that you already know you are receiving. For example, if you want a cappuccino machine, and your Aunt Harriet already promised you one, then you will not want to list that. This is your wish list only.

Registering for Gifts

Now that you've taken a general inventory and decided what you need for your new home, take this list with you when you register for gifts. If you have friends and family out of state, consider registering at two or three retailers, at least one of which is nationwide. Make sure whatever retailer you choose offers easy returns and exchanges so you won't get stuck with five woks. Be sure to register for gifts in a range of prices so all guests can find items they can afford. The more items you receive as wedding gifts that are things you really need, the less you will have to spend *after* the wedding to set up your home. Only register for things you'll really use. If you're not a china and crystal type, don't feel obligated to register for these. You can choose practical or recreational items such as furniture and tools or even camping gear and board games. With careful planning, you can avoid owning a cabinet full of rarely used silver platters and crystal goblets, while having to spend hundreds of dollars on practical necessities— like a vacuum cleaner, gas grill, or mixing bowls that you overlooked when registering. This will help reduce some of the financial stress that most newlyweds face in their first year together.

Bridal Showers

When you are given a bridal shower by one of your wedding party attendants, your aunt, your place of employment, or your classmates from school, remember that giving out a list of desired gifts is appropriate only if asked, but most hostesses will ask you for this list and for the places you are registered. Keep in mind that if these shower guests are invited to the wedding as well as the shower, there is no obligation to give two separate gifts. Be sure to give them an up-to-date list of the items you truly need. I can't tell you how many showers I've attended and watched as an uncomfortable bride-to-be unwraps two and even three of the same gift—even though the obviously frustrated guests consulted the registry before purchasing. Update your gift registry regularly and try to choose a retailer that does as well. A couple of months ago I went to a Target gift registry and it automatically updated the items on a national computer as they were purchased. Plus they issued a duplicate receipt (without the price on it) to include with the gift in the event the bride needed to return the item.

If you are given a lingerie shower, guests should, of course, have the option to purchase any gift they choose. However, if the hostess asks you for your preferred style of lingerie, be sure to ask for bras and undies that are your style and size and not just for exciting nighties. How many of those little nothings do you REALLY need? Why not include a specific swimsuit, linen sprays and body lotion (specify scents), or a robe and slippers you like? Sometimes a lot of money is spent on lingerie showers, and the bride-to-be ends up with fifteen little nothings that she'll likely wear for a brief (pardon the pun) period of time. By being specific and practical, you'll have enough lingerie to last the first year.

The Empire State Building Revisited

There's one other lesson to be learned from this chapter's opening story. We can overcome almost anything for love. Bob overcame his fear and he was well rewarded by a grateful wife. I knew I'd use that story for this book because it was so romantic; I even thought of writing the story *before* we visited New York City, but realized we'd be acting from a script if I did so—

and life isn't scripted. The wedding, like the marriage, is going to be about give and take. If your focus is on your future mate rather than your own agenda, then you will be laying the foundations for a profitable and pleasurable life together.

Don't expect life to be like the movies, and you'll be fine.

CHAPTER 2

"FAAST, WE CHAZ THE WADDING CAAK, MR. BAANKS!"

Maximizing Your Wedding Without Borrowing on Your Future

If you haven't seen the remake of the classic movie *Father of the Bride* (FOTB), drop everything, rent the video, and watch it tonight! Actually, the original, starring Elizabeth Taylor and Spencer Tracy, as well as the remake starring Steve Martin and Diane Keaton, should be required viewing for all brides-to-be in my book. And since this *is* my book—you are required to see these movies!

In the new version of FOTB, there's the priceless scene where the daughter first tells her dad she's engaged. She is just recently back from a trip to Rome and she's sitting at the dinner table with her family as she struggles to explain:

"You see, I met this guy ... and he's completely wonderful. He's a lot like Dad, actually. Well, we fell in love, and ... we've decided to get married." Her countenance glows with the wonder of it all as she exclaims, "I'm engaged! Ahhh! Can you believe it? I'm getting married!" She wiggles in her seat like a giddy schoolgirl.

At this point, George Banks looks at his daughter and does a double take. Instead of seeing his adult daughter, he sees his seven-year-old little girl with brown pigtails and red ribbons in her hair. She speaks to him in an angelic voice, "Dad, I met a man in Rome, and he's wonderful and he's brilliant and we're getting married."

When we first watched this movie on video, Bethany was only about five years old. One day shortly after Bob and I had seen the movie, I braided Bethany's hair so that she looked like the little girl in the movie. I thought I would have a little fun at Bob's expense. So that night when he came home from work, Bethany sat at the dinner table and on my silent cue announced with sincerity, "Papa, I met a man in Rome, we fell in love, and I'm going to get married."

It was soooo cute that I just knew Bob would love how sweetly Bethany could reenact that scene. Well, I found out I didn't know Bob as well as I thought!

When Bethany said her line, Bob put down his fork and looked up in bewilderment. The expression on his face indicated that his mind was fast-forwarding about twenty years—and he didn't like what he saw: his precious little "Bunny" all grown up and leaving her Papa. He shuddered at the thought and shook his bewildered head as he groused, "That's *not* funny. That's not funny at all."

A scene that Bob enjoyed a lot more is when George reluctantly tags along with his wife and daughter to visit an effeminate wedding coordinator named Franc. Things get interesting when Franc's thick foreign accent gums up his English. He fluidly converses in a lingo that everyone seems to understand but George.

"I sugoost we paack the caak. The caak dattamines the kand of wadding you vill be haffing. So we shaad faast pick the caak," Franc says to the father of the bride, who just sits there with a look of utter confusion on his face, while his wife and daughter smile, nod, and eagerly reply, "O-kaay."

George says, "What? I think I missed that."

The mother and daughter are visibly embarrassed by George's ineptitude. "The *cake,* George," his wife prods while his daughter adds, "Franc wants us to pick out the wedding cake first, Dad."

The two scenes I described above have one major thing in common: wedding-planning oftentimes elicits a variety of emotions that can be confusing at times. Consequently, tempers may flare at the least provocation or tears can flow at something as innocuous as a *Hallmark* commercial. It's important to realize that there will be ups and downs in this great roller coaster ride—but it will be worth it in the end.

You can still have your wedding cake, and eat it too.

It's a proven fact that if you can minimize the financial stress of planning a wedding, you will greatly minimize the overall stress. In a nutshell: If you stay on budget, you won't be so uptight. Contrary to what you might think, you can still have your wedding cake and eat it too. You don't have to turn the reception into a potluck dinner or hand deliver all your invitations in order to save money! You can have elegance without extra expense. This chapter will give you some ideas to consider that will help you keep these expenses to a minimum.

Plan Ahead

The sooner you can sit down and plan your budget as outlined in chapter 1, the better off you'll be financially. Now is a good time to generate a "to-do" list that is customized according to your needs. Planning information and scheduling tools are available online, such as the twelve-month countdown checklist at *weddingchannel.com*. Or, if you choose to purchase a planner, I would recommend *The Christian Wedding Planner* (Bethany House Publishers, 2003). It's a gorgeous, oversized, full-color book with a number of great features. It is not only a planner but also a keepsake of your wedding. Another good resource to look at early is by H. Norman Wright called *The Complete Book of Christian Wedding Vows* (Bethany House Publishers, 2001). This book is essentially for customizing one of the most personal parts of the ceremony.

Now let's get back to the financial aspect of planning. Not only will you know what you can spend but you will also have a pretty good idea of the items you will need to collect. For example, if you have decided to use silk flowers and have a relative who has a knack for floral arranging, you can begin to look for sales at craft and hobby stores. Once you buy something, make a note of it on your master list, because in the flurry of prenuptial bliss, it's easy to forget you already bought the ring pillow or the bridal guest book when you found them on sale.

Save receipts on EVERYTHING you buy and put them in a file folder. Do not unwrap items until you absolutely have to. That way, if Uncle Fester decides to buy you a 24K gold-plated cake server, then you can take back the one you bought on sale. Organization is often the key to major savings.

The Hope Chest

When I was twelve years old, my Great-Grandma Laudeman gave me a one-hundred-year-old hope chest. It was pieced together using wooden pegs, and I will give it to my daughter Bethany when she turns twelve. If you don't already have one of these American traditions, put together your own "Wedding Box." This is where you'll put the items you've collected and added to your master list so that you'll be organized and have everything in one general area. Your makeshift hope chest can be as simple as a large plastic storage container, and you should have one for each of the following categories (contents are only suggestions; not all brides will use all items mentioned):

Pre-Wedding Everything you will need to have in place *before* the wedding ceremony: shoes, hose, jewelry, special makeup, outfit to wear for honeymoon departure, gifts for attendants, checks for the musicians and pastor, CDs, invitation list, invitations, return labels, stamps, directions to reception and church, requirements for organist or pianist, cake ordering options, etc. Most brides don't pick up their dress from the boutique until right before the wedding—this lessens the chance of it getting crushed or wrinkled. If your gown is a preexisting one or is being stored until the wedding, consider having a professional cleaner or bridal boutique steam the gown the day before the wedding. Ironing a wedding gown can leave disastrous scorch marks.

Wedding These are things that will be used on the wedding day for the actual ceremony. These include the guest registry, pen, decorations, ring pillow and rings, any silk flowers for bouquets, hair decorations, corsages, boutonnieres, church decorations, ceremony program, wedding Bible, memory book, etc.

Reception Everything you'll need immediately after the ceremony and before the honeymoon goes in this box. If the caterer or person in charge of the reception does not already provide plates, napkins, and utensils, these will need to be collected. Also includes meal menu, cake server, champagne or punch for toasting and special glasses, garter, band arrangements and requirements, rice or birdseed packets, gift list, etc.

Honeymoon Gather what you will need for the honeymoon: travel itinerary, tickets, passports (if required), camera, swimsuits, lingerie, special gift for hubby, candles, lotion, bubble bath, etc.—a packed bag or two.

Post-Wedding Even after the wedding and honeymoon are over, you will need thank-you notes, addresses, stamps, duplicate gifts to return, and receipts (if available).

With This Ring, I Thee Wed

If your fiancé hasn't already placed the ring on your finger, remember that your ring is something you will have long after the gown is in storage and the flowers have faded—so you'll want to carefully consider before purchasing yours.

Choose a ring that suits your hand and lifestyle. Find a balance between a Zsa Zsa Gabor diamond and a plain gold band. If you have a job that is hard on the hands, then a simple gold band might be the best option. Try on various styles, not just your preconceived notion of "the perfect ring." This is often how the best matches are found.

Two months salary? Ads try to tell you how much you should spend on a diamond engagement ring. Salespeople may try to pressure you to spend more in order to buy a diamond of a certain size. You may believe that diamonds are a sound investment; but remember that retailers usually mark up a new diamond ring by as much as 100 percent. It could lose half its value the moment you leave the shop. Buy smart, and spend only what you can realistically afford. "Diamonds are forever," but you don't want to be *paying* for yours forever.

You may want to ask your jeweler if they will allow you to trade up at any time. There are many stores that allow this service as long as you keep your receipt. So if you cannot afford the ring you'd really like now and you're not willing to go into debt for it, then purchasing through a vendor with these policies will allow for a future trade up.

You might also think long range in terms of a wedding anniversary band. You may want to pick a style that will coordinate with a five- or ten-year diamond anniversary band that you can add later to enhance the look of a simple ring.

If you were given a family ring, but you're not crazy about the setting, then you might consider having a new setting made. You'll have the sentimental value of the ring by using the stones and the uniqueness of your own ring with your selected setting. One friend told me that she agonized over how to tell her boyfriend that she already had a diamond ring without sounding like she was presuming he was going to ask her to marry him. "I knew he was getting close to proposing, and I didn't want him to go out and buy a diamond when I already had my grandmother's one-carat solitaire." One evening she sputtered nervously, "I'm not presuming that you are going to ... but if you are, I don't want you to go out and buy one when I already have one ..."

Her dear one interrupted gently, asking, "Honey, what are you talking about?" Giving up, she went to her dresser and retrieved the diamond ring and thrust it, embarrassed, into his hands. Delighted, he strutted into work the next day, announcing, "Yep, she gave me the ring last night."

Together they picked out a lovely new setting for the diamond. She was happy to wear her grandmother's diamond, and you can bet he didn't mind getting a gorgeous ring so inexpensively.

Don't think you can only buy from a jeweler; consider reputable department stores as well. They run some fabulous sales and clearances that can save you as much as 50 percent. They will also guarantee the quality of the diamond. This ring could go on a layaway plan so that you will not go into debt. If you're not certain about the quality of the diamond, be sure you can return the ring. Take it to a jeweler for verification of the quality of the stone. Be sure to get the appraised value of the ring for insurance purposes. If the ring is valued more than the maximum jewelry limitation on your policy, you will need to get it put on a schedule for the actual replacement value on your homeowner's policy or tenant policy.

"Diamonds are forever," but you don't want to be *paying* for yours forever.

Here are some further tips on selecting a diamond from the EGL USA (European Gemological Laboratory):

Date of Report. There's a possibility that the diamond has been damaged since the report was issued. Ask your retailer to show you that your diamond matches the report.

Identification Number. Consumers can check out individual certificates online via *www.EGLUSA.com*. Often this identification number can be found laser-inscribed on the diamond itself. If your stone doesn't have an inscribed number, ask your jeweler to have it done.

It's the genuine article. Look for a statement that says that the diamond is genuine and whether it has been enhanced—meaning if it has been treated to fill fractures. Labs will not grade fracture-filled diamonds, though reports are issued about laser-drilled diamonds.

Weight. The exact carat measurement must appear on the report.

Shape and cut. The stone's shape (round, pear, oval) and its cutting style (brilliant or step-cut) are noted on the certificate.

Measurements. Most labs measure diamonds in millimeters, most often to the hundredth. These exact dimensions are important for identification; it's unlikely that two diamonds will have identical weight and dimensions.

Proportion. Good proportion, especially the depth and table percentages, affects the brilliance and fire of a diamond. Proportion may be as important as color and clarity grades, says EGL USA.

Clarity and color grades. Learn the "4 C's." Don't even think about shopping until you've done your homework and memorized the 4 C's: Clarity, Color, Cut, and Carat (weight).

Contact Info. A few hours of research now will save you hundreds if not thousands of dollars in the end. For further tips about selecting a diamond, visit the Web site of the EGL USA or call toll-free 877-EGL-USA1 and ask for their diamond buyer's guide. Other helpful Web sites include: *www.bridaltips.com/diamond.htm* and *www.weddingplanning.com/tips/wedding_rings.html.*

"Going to the Chapel, and We're Gonna Get Married!"

The first major consideration in planning the wedding is *where* you are going to get married and where you will have the reception. The cost for these arrangements can range anywhere from $0 to $10,000 and should be considered part of the budget for the wedding. This can be one of those "hidden expenses" that you don't plan on unless you're careful.

The obvious choice is your local church, but if it only accommodates two hundred people in the chapel, and you are expecting three hundred guests, then you will have to look elsewhere.

Some of the considerations for non-church weddings could include a beautiful home that has a lovely garden and a huge great room as a back up in the event of rain. (When we were in Columbus, Mississippi, there was a GORGEOUS mansion called "Bryn Bella" that looked like "Tara" from *Gone With the Wind,* and people rented it out on occasion.) Have you seen the *Funniest Home Videos* show on weddings? I'll never forget the one that featured an outside wedding: a deluge rain shower collapsed the tents that had been set up in the event of rain. That was not a pretty picture. It left the poor bride sobbing and the groom (whose idea it was) baffled.

Other couples have chosen upscale, well-landscaped hotels, clubs, or restaurants that also serve as the site for the reception. At the less expensive end of the spectrum are rental halls, community centers, or university or publicly owned buildings. If you simply can't agree on any of this wedding stuff, there's always Las Vegas and its many "Chapels o' Love." Make a list of options and make it a part of date night with your fiancé to check them out and choose one together.

Come One, Come All! (But Only If You Have an Invitation)

What's a party without the guests? Remember that many of your guests will have a spouse or significant other and will count for two people. For single people, be sure to address the invitation to "So-and-so and guest." This eliminates confusion for the invitee. Otherwise, only the people listed on the invitation are expected to come. Keep in mind that the more people you invite, the more expensive your wedding will be. You can keep track of everyone through the convenient "Guest List Manager" at *http://wedding.weddingchannel.com/pwp/ww_sell.asp.*

That site mentions: "One smart planning tip is to have a 'must-have' A-list and a 'would-like-to-include' B-list, and mail your invitations early. If some A-list guests can't make it, you can mail out invitations to B-list guests, and they won't feel like last-minute additions. The only real downside to this approach is the risk of hurt feelings if a guest realizes he or she wasn't on the first list. To avoid this, make sure nothing on the invitation or envelope indicates A or B, and don't send out any invitations too close to the wedding date." If you're still staying up late worrying about whom to invite, have everyone who submitted names to your list prioritize them in rank order. Once you get close to your cut-off limit, you will have the names ready to eliminate.

The invitation does more than invite people to your celebration; it serves as the "first impression" for the value you've placed on this special day. I've seen computer-generated invitations that would cost only slightly less than the simplest invitation from a professional printer, and they scream, "Cheez Whiz will be served at the reception!" To save money, consider using the less-than-deluxe version of a professionally printed invitation rather than something that looks homemade. I need to add a caveat, however, and that is if you or a friend is design savvy, there are some great computer programs out there for designing invitations, programs, etc. If you use quality-weight paper, and a laser printer, do-it-yourself invitations can look quite nice.

If you are considering ordering through a professional wedding planner, keep in mind that he or she is out to make money, just like any other business. The same holds true for bridal Web sites, which make commissions on each registry and referral. So choose carefully. Consequently, there can be quite a few add-on costs. When you look at a sample book from your printer, note the style number, the manufacturer, and the price. Don't order your invitations on the same day until you've gone home and looked up the manufacturer's Web site to see if they have a better price there. If the price is lower, print out the page and take it back to your local printer to see if they will match that price.

> For budgeting purposes, you can safely assume that about 60 to 70 percent of your invited guests will attend the wedding and reception.

More and more people are forgoing the return card for the reception because so many people do not return them. Many are requesting RSVPs via voice mail or e-mail instead. For budgeting purposes, you can safely assume that about 60 to 70 percent of your invited guests will attend the wedding and reception. Don't e-mail invitations and don't announce that you'll accept cash instead of gifts on the invitation. (Don't laugh, I've seen both, and they were shocking.) But do set up a Web site for your wedding and place the address on the invitations. Set aside enough money in your invitation budget to mail them. Some families hand deliver invitations. However, a mailed card is the protocol for a formal event. A mailed thank-you note also tells the recipient that their gift was worth the cost and effort to mail the thank-you.

Wedding Web Site

Consider setting up a simple Web site either off an existing Web site you may have or by creating a new one. A couple of options that exist already are: *http://wedding.*

weddingchannel.com/pwp/ww_sell.asp and *www.theknot.com*. This site can be updated the closer you get to the wedding, and you should put the Web site address on your invitations. Post invitation information at the site, including maps to the church and reception. You can list your registry information as well.

Smile, You're on Candid Camera!

Many couples try to save money in this critical area. However, if you marked "memories" as high on your list of priorities for the exercise in chapter 1, you'll realize that photography is not the area to scrimp on. Having that "great" amateur photographer from the mailroom at work memorialize one of the most important days of your life is simply *not* worth the risk!

Brian Shul, a professional wedding photographer and author of many books featuring his photographs, is also a friend of ours. When he realized I was writing this book, he said:

> Ellie, my main message to new brides is NOT to try to save money on the photography, but to devote a good amount to insure you are getting someone reputable. I do tell them they don't have to spend $3,000, though, as there are many overpriced guys out there that really don't take enough pictures. They need to make an informed choice on their photographer so that they don't regret it for the rest of their lives. Brides get very much into the gown and waste huge amounts on the reception, never realizing throughout the process how important their pictures are going to be later. So many of them think that Uncle Harry can do the pictures. But he doesn't understand anything about lighting inside the church or dealing with shadows outside.

Ask to see some of the photographer's work and for references. Then do your research by calling these previous clients and asking them the following questions:

1. Were you satisfied with the quality and content of your photos?
2. Do you feel you were overcharged for the work?
3. Do you think you'll still be satisfied with these photos twenty years from now?

4. Was the photographer good with people, relaxed in getting them to cooperate and smile? (It's important that a photographer is a good people person.)
5. Were you given a financial estimate, and did the finished work exceed that?
6. What was the price of your package? (Try to make sure you get at least as good a deal as they got.)

The same principles apply to hiring a wedding videographer. Again, avoid the temptation to save money by letting your husband's buddy videotape the wedding. This happened at a friend's wedding, and she ended up with such a dark video that all you can see of the ceremony are the candles flickering and the ghostly white of her dress and veil—the invisible bride! Interview professional videographers, get the costs up front, references, and view samples of their work. Most videographers should be secured quite early in the engagement because many are now covering pre-wedding aspects of the event as well, including interviews with the bride, groom, and extended members of the family. Some will even follow you to the florist and bakery when you order these items for the event. Keep in mind that these people will probably cover EVERYTHING on video. But the upside to that is, if the elastic in Aunt Harriet's pantyhose gives way, you could possibly send the video to Hollywood and win $10,000!

The Bridal Gown, Bridesmaids' and Flower Girl's Gowns

A friend of mine was helping her beautiful future daughter-in-law shop for her wedding gown. This stunning girl came out in a simple yet elegant gown, and every eye in the showroom turned to admire her. Then the salesclerk showed her a magnificent gown that cost almost four times as much. Knowing this was way out of her price range, the bride-to-be declined to try it on. But my friend was willing to splurge and make up the difference if the bride really wanted the gown. So the young lady tried it on. Once again, every eye turned to admire the result of the gorgeous girl in a magnificent gown.

When it came time to decide on the purchase, the salesclerk called them aside: "I know that I should probably talk you into the most expensive gown, but I have to tell you that when you wore it, every eye was on the *gown*. But when you came out in the simpler gown—every eye was on the *bride*." Guess which gown they selected?

In order to keep from being upstaged by the bridal gown that may cost several thousand dollars, consider these less expensive alternatives instead:

Family Heirloom Gown   Of course the best savings is to pay nothing at all, to have a gown that has been in the family and would provide the added value of family memories and history. This could be a gown worn (and possibly altered) from the bride or groom's mother, grandmother, aunt, or sister.

Consignment   It's obvious that most bridal gowns in these shops have been worn once, but some are never worn at all for various reasons. Check the newspaper Want Ads and look in the Yellow Pages for consignment stores that feature bridal wear. It might even be worth it to go to a nearby larger city that would have a greater selection. Be sure to check seams, beading, and other detail work. If you bring along a family member or friend who has some knowledge of sewing, they can tell you whether a gown can be altered to fit you or if damaged beading can be adequately repaired. You could find a much nicer gown this way for less money that will still keep the focus on the bride.

Custom Tailored   A handmade gown will likely be more expensive than a dress purchased on consignment, but of course the advantage is that it will be new. Before you decide to have a gown made, here are a few precautions. First, make sure the seamstress is reputable. Ask for references and to see some of her work. If a family member wants to make your gown, realize that you will likely feel obligated to wear it—even if it ends up looking like Olive Oyl's nightgown. Secondly, realize that quality fabric and notions—beading, lace, etc.—are very expensive. Add up all of the materials before you decide. Handmade may be a better option for the bridesmaids' dresses, which are uniform but are not as intricate and involved.

Timing   The best time to shop for bridesmaids' gowns, mothers' gowns, and even some nontraditional wedding gowns, would be right after prom season or right after the Christmas holidays. If the colors and styles are right for your wedding party, you could save as much as 75 percent on clearance items.

Flower Girl A favorite part of any wedding is watching the cute little flower girl. Since all eyes will be on the little darling, a simple dress will usually suffice. For these gowns, in particular, you could shop off the rack at discount department stores and happen upon quite a cute find.

Alterations One of the prettiest gowns I ever saw on a bride was also the most amazing when I found out where it came from. She started with a simple dress and then transformed it into a princess gown by adding new sleeves, beading, and a train! The alterations were done by a professional, and the final cost was still less than an equally beautiful gown from a bridal boutique.

Bridal Boutiques As soon as you go into one of these stores, head to the back where the clearance section is, but be careful! When you walk in, it's easy to lose your head and bust your budget on the "perfect" dress. Remember what you've budgeted for the dress compared to the other wedding expenses. You don't want to end up spending 80 percent of your budget on the dress and end up eating saltines and Uncle Louie's hot sauce at the reception! If you find a dress you just love at a boutique—and it fits—ask about buying the sample dress at a reduced price.

Bridal Warehouses You can often find good deals on gowns at bridal warehouses or outlets (they even have occasional sales where many dresses are marked down to $99). Warehouses don't offer the same level of personal attention as boutiques, but they do offer significant savings. And since the gowns are sold off the rack, there's no need to order and then wait months to receive your dress.

Shoes Remember the shoes are mostly hidden by the dress and will likely only be used once, so don't overspend. Payless Shoe Source usually has coupons at their Web site, and they carry dyeable shoes. Look for "buy one, get one free" shoes, and you can purchase your bridal shoes and honeymoon outfit shoes in the same purchase.

Don't be locked into dyeable shoes either. Some high-heeled styles might work nicely (but not too high, or you might make an unexpected train trip!). For bridesmaids' shoes, you can also be creative. If the dresses have gold or silver accents, you may be able to find shoes to match those colors. Or ask your bridesmaids to purchase any shoe they like in a basic coordinating color, such as white or black patent.

Prince Charming

For many men, this is the only time in their lives they'd be caught wearing a tux—so be sure you have a good photographer! Military weddings are the least expensive, because the groom and his attendants can all be in uniform (and have a wonderful sword bridge as well). But for the rest of you, go to my Web site at *www.elliekay.com* and link onto sites such as *coolsavings.com* and *valupage.com* for specific tux rental deals in your area. Some men buy black suits and rent only a contrasting color tuxedo vest and shirt, saving a considerable amount of money and allowing them the future use of the suit. For a less traditional look, some weddings have incorporated a western motif. The important thing is that you and your fiancé agree on the style that your wedding will have and plan accordingly.

> Go to *www.elliekay.com* and link onto sites such as *coolsavings.com* and *valupage.com* for specific tux rental deals in your area.

What to Do With Your 'Do

Most men only have to get out of bed, wash their hair, and comb it. Women, however, have to wash, dry, curl, dye, style, and fret over their locks. Look through the books your stylist has and decide what kind of a look you want. Hair up and pulled back provides a classic look for years to come.

Be sure to go to a stylist you trust and also trust her judgment as to whether the style you select will really work with your face, veil, and dress. One of my friends thought the style she chose would make her look stunning; instead it made her look like she had a pineapple crown on her head! She was so glad she went for a trial run before the big event.

Take the veil with you so your stylist can work with it ahead of time. Some weddings have everyone in a French braid or up-do to match and coordinate. But you will need to confer with the other attendants before you mandate anything. Remember that the more difficult the up-do, such as a French twist, the harder it will be to replicate in the event that your stylist is late or someone's hair falls down. One final effect is to place small and simple silk or fresh flowers in the hairstyle to adorn it, but be sure to practice this ahead of time as well.

Best Face Forward

The same principles apply to letting a beautician put on your makeup. You may end up looking like a court jester instead of a blushing bride. Here are some basic tips for wedding day makeup:

- Use natural-looking foundation that conceals imperfections and matches your skin tone; blend well at jawline.
- Dust with powder to keep down shine.
- Lightly apply eyeliner—brown is good. Avoid raccoon eyes!
- Use mascara; it will frame and brighten your eyes in your photographs.
- Don't be afraid to use a shade of lipstick that is *slightly* more vivid than your everyday color. Otherwise, your lips may look "washed out" under photographer's lights.
- Avoid anything green (eye shadow or liner); it tends to look harsh under artificial light.

Tiptoe Through the Tulips

Flowers are usually the biggest sticker shock for novice wedding planners. Fresh flowers and professional arrangements are the most expensive option. The best course of action is to decide before you go into a shop how many corsages, bouquets, and floral arrangements you will need. If you have everything written down, you're less likely to be swayed by someone who is doing their job in the floral shop—selling flowers, and lots of them. If you must have fresh, choose locally grown and in-season flowers, and less expensive fillers like baby's breath or ivy. Or instead of a large bouquet, consider a single or trio of large, stunning blooms, like calla lilies or sunflowers.

Remember that most churches have an assortment of dried arrangements already in their storage rooms. Ask to see these before you decide on what flowers you will need. You might have to have these arrangements professionally cleaned—but that will still cost less than an entirely new arrangement.

The least expensive option is usually silk flowers made by someone in your family who is gifted at this and can help you develop the arrangements you want. If you have adequate storage space, these can be done months in advance and crossed off your list early. Bouquets and boutonnieres are the easiest to do, and the supplies for these are as near as your closest Wal-Mart. They sell bouquet holders that are white, but can easily be spray-painted the desired color.

Boutonniere holders may be purchased in advance and then fresh flowers added when they are assembled a day or two before the event. To assemble them, just add the fresh flower, some dried baby's breath, one or two extra green leaves from the bouquets, and bind them with green florist's tape. Be sure you don't get the bloom too big or your husband's attendants will look like they're wearing homecoming corsages!

Receptions With Food, Family, Friends, and Fun

As Brian Shul said earlier in the chapter, receptions are one area where you can get carried away. I have found that it's usually the bride's or groom's family that starts to go wild when planning for the reception. I knew one father of the bride who spent all his daughter's college money (she got married before she finished school) on a fancy wedding at a country club that neither the bride nor groom wanted. This man carried around photos of the ice sculpture, steamship round of beef, and the wedding cake for months—showing anyone who didn't care to see it! His daughter and new husband had the financial burden of college, but the dad got the reception of his dreams.

Here are a few quick tips to cut costs at receptions:

- Order half the napkins with your names on them and half with the reception colors of choice. Alternate these on the table.
- Use rose petals for decorations on the tables. Many florists will give you free petals, and even buying roses to get the petals costs less than other decorating options.
- Depending on the time of year, you can use ivy, holly, or flowers from family gardens.
- Church fellowship halls are usually free, but some have restrictions on the kind of music that can be played or whether champagne can be served.
- View the facilities and look over details. While you may not be able to afford the prettiest place in town, you don't want to pay for ugly or a room that is in disrepair.
- Consider hiring an award-winning quartet from the local high school or community college. Oftentimes these groups are looking for the opportunity to perform before competition and you can make a donation to their school. But be sure you listen to them first before booking them. My son Philip is a cellist, and they've played at wedding receptions with rave reviews. Get guarantees from their instructor that they will be there and be on time. You'll also need to provide food for them after the reception as a courtesy.
- If you hire a DJ, be sure to select the specific CDs and songs you will and will not want played. Also get a referral from other jobs he's done and try to watch him in action one time. If the DJ is a microphone hog, he can ruin the event for everyone. However, if he's experienced in weddings, he can bring just the right amount of fun to the event and can help ease any residual tension that is left over from the ceremony. Remember that you can request theme music: love songs from the '50s, big band swing music from the '40s, or even disco from the '80s.
- Veggie platters last longer (so there's still food on the table) and cost less than fruit, meat, or cheese. So order extra of these in addition to your other needs.
- Buffets cost less. If possible, reserve the "sit-down dinner" for the rehearsal dinner and not the reception, unless you have an above-average amount to spend.

- Receptions themed around Mexican or Chinese food often cost less than fancy finger foods or hors d'oeuvres.
- Consider a dessert reception, appetizer-only reception, or brunch (if your wedding can be planned for the morning), which can be less expensive than a full dinner menu.
- If a family member offers to do the catering, go over a menu with them and a time schedule (if food is to be prepared ahead of time and frozen). Also be sure that they have a history of being reliable, because the fallout of a poorly organized reception is just not worth the money saved.

Let 'Em Eat Cake

Speaking of cake, I'd like to close out this chapter with another vignette from *Father of the Bride*. George Banks is discussing the price of his daughter's wedding cake with Franc.

"Is that in *dollars*?" he asks Franc incredulously.

Franc, in a condescending tone, replies, "Haa, Maaster Baanks! Velcome to da twenty-fast santury!"

Well, you don't have to pay $1,400 for a cake in order to "arrive" in our new millennium. On the other hand, you don't want someone to offer to make the cake in order to save money and then have it fall in half off the table (I've seen this happen too). So there's a balance between quality and frugality that should be kept in mind. Go to one of the wedding sites we've already listed and look at the photos of cakes. Pick one you like and take it to several of your local bakeries for a bid. People can detect a homemade cake from miles away, and you do want a professional look. The same would apply for a groom's cake, which is an optional cake dedicated to the groom. Another option is to order a smaller decorated cake for the cake cutting and supplement it with sheet cakes of the same flavor to be cut in the kitchen for the guests.

You should figure on cake for 60 percent of the general invitation list (if you do not have RSVPs) or 100 percent of the confirmed attendees because people tend to bring dates, kids, or others to a wedding (unless it is a sit-down reception). The groom's cake should be half the size of the primary wedding cake and it is usually chocolate. Be sure you sample the bakery's other cakes to make sure it is of good quality.

Just Married

Once the wedding and reception are over, you'll be ready to head off to your honeymoon. Remember that the "happily ever after" is the reason you got married—not so you could blow your life savings on a one-day extravaganza. You and your fiancé are taking this big step because you love each other—not because you love event planning!

CHAPTER 3

THE HONEYMOONERS

Don't touch my wife!"

The tall, dark, handsome man took one step backward and looked at the man who had just spoken those threatening words. He couldn't determine whether they were said in jest or with serious intention. He glanced again at the man who had uttered the warning and decided he wasn't going to find out!

How to Have a Fabulous

Trip on a Shoestring

The tall man was Bob's best friend, Mike. The younger man was Bob, and the occasion was our honeymoon. Mike had just "kissed the bride," since he couldn't make it to the wedding. I learned quickly that every time another man gives me a hug, a social kiss on the cheek (as they do in some military circles), or a playful pat on the arm—Bob will always say,

"Don't touch my wife!"

And the guys, old and young alike, usually aren't quite sure if he's joking.

I sometimes wonder myself.

Over the years Bob has occasionally had to modify those words, especially when a General has just kissed my cheek at a social gathering. In that case, his tone is a bit friendlier as he says: "Don't touch my wife, *sir*."

But you have to wonder.

One day recently we were in the Officer's Club watching the fighter

pilots play a game called "Crud" on a snooker table. It's a complicated, high-contact game played with a cue ball and a striped ball around a pool table. It has lots of silly rules that make tempers flare. The macho factor is usually pretty high during a Crud tournament, and it was particularly high on this night.

I love Crud. I love to watch it and I love to play it. My call sign is "Miss Ellie," and I'm fairly aggressive. But there's one thing I'm not and that's macho. There weren't any women playing in this particular tournament (although we've played *and won* in the past), so I was relegated to the sidelines.

The 8th Squadron, or Black Sheep, were in the finals with the Flying Knights of the 9th Squadron, and I was standing right by the action discussing the finer points of the game with K–9 (the call sign for Bob's squadron commander). Bob was getting me a Diet Coke while a dispute of a "bad call" was going on by the table.

About that time, Tim, a neighbor of ours, walked up to K–9 to ask what they were arguing about. But before K–9 could explain, Tim saw me and reached over to give me a kiss on the cheek and say "hello." Suddenly, from out of nowhere, a voice bellowed out:

"Don't touch my wife!"

Tim, who is a good four inches shorter than Bob, looked over at him while K–9 tried to figure out if Bob was just joking or if there was going to be a fight breaking out in this fine establishment.

Tim was nonplussed by Bob's threatening words, and he quickly replied, "What? Hey, I'll kiss you too!" and before anyone could react, Tim kissed Bob on the cheek—with Italian gusto.

I laughed out loud and so did Bob—it was outrageous!

K–9 was not all that convinced that guys should be kissing each other in this environment, and his face registered shock, disbelief, and then mild amusement. He stuck his hand out toward Bob while shooting a wary glance at Tim: "I think I'll just shake your hand instead."

The game was back in action again as we laughed at Tim's "in your face" humor. But before we gave Crud our full attention again, K–9 turned back around to Bob one last time: "Don't worry, Bob. I didn't touch your wife."

Things can change dramatically once the "I do's" have been said and the rice is shaken out of your pockets. Guys sometimes get more protective of their spouses, and thus we begin the journey of establishing trust and defining acceptable social mores for our married life. But before we have to face the stark realities of building a compatible life together, we get to do something as outrageously fun as Tim's antics—we get to go on a honeymoon!

This is a time to share intimate moments together mixed with large doses of memory-making fun. Remember that you never get a second chance to take a first honeymoon—no matter how much you can afford to spend. So it's really important that you make this unique time something special, fun, and memorable.

This chapter is filled with tons of great ideas to get twice the trip out of half the funds. There are also ideas to keep the honeymoon going with all kinds of inexpensive travel and entertainment.

Airfares

Check out the fares available on the Internet such as *www.bestfares.com*, *www.expedia.com* or 800–397–3342, *www.smarterliving.com*, and *www.cheaptickets.com*.

Once you find the best fares at some of these Web sites, be sure to go back to the original airline's site to check for even better deals. For example, I checked a fare to go see my publisher in Minneapolis and found a ticket (normally $800) on *expedia.com* for only $325 on Frontier Airlines. But when I went to the Frontier site, I found an unadvertised fare for only $200. The Expedia fare alerted me to the airline to check for that particular flight. Read on for the details.

Airline Internet Specials

One final tip is to try the airlines directly for their Internet specials. Most major U.S. carriers offer these weekly specials. You can try American Airlines' Net SAAvers at *www.aa.com*, U.S.

Airways' E-Savers at *www.usairways.com*, United's E-Fares at *www.ual.com*, or Northwest Airlines' CyberSavers at *www.nwa.com*. I tried Southwest Airlines at *www.southwestairlines.com* for their Click 'n Save Specials. I just booked two round-trip, nonstop tickets from El Paso to Dallas for a total of $220 (only $110 each). The catch is that you have to buy well in advance, and they are nonrefundable and no changes can be made. There are no reserved seats on this airline, but that is why they have some of the cheapest fares in the industry. If you get to the gate about an hour and fifteen minutes ahead of departure time, you can be one of the first people on the plane and get a comfortable seat in the bulkhead area (unless there are handicapped individuals flying, who have priority). These flights are usually booked, which is why it's important to book them early.

Online Auctions and *Priceline.com*

While dot.com businesses tend to come and go, it seems likely that travel sites and online auctions will survive because people are getting good bargains and are willing to continue to use these services in order to get (and sell) the trips they want. Online auction sites for airline tickets and other travel needs tend to be low on service but high on value. Look for established sites such as *www.ebay.com*, *www.skyauction.com*, or *www.bidtripper.com* for some good values. You can get half-price hotels, rental cars, plane tickets, entertainment tickets, etc. You will need to do your research on the balance of a good airfare with a good hotel rate. For example, even though airfare to Chicago can be cheap (they have two major airports, served by dozens of airlines), city hotel costs can be steep. Finding a cheaper hotel at an auction and the airfare at a travel site could be the best value.

Priceline.com is unique from other auction sites because no one bids against you—they just let you know if you can have the price you bid. Some people love Priceline and others are very disappointed. If you're going to use it, you will need to keep the following things in mind:

- Do your research on the lowest fare you can find and plan to bid about 20 percent lower than that fare. If you don't get the bid, you've lost nothing.
- Have your credit card ready.

- Enter your destination, departing and arrival airports, and dates of departure and arrival.
- Enter your price bid.
- Remember these are nonrefundable, and you cannot control the departure or arrival times.
- Usually within twenty-four hours you'll have an acceptance or rejection.
- If you are rejected, *you cannot enter the same information with a higher price!* You will have to change one of the pieces of information listed: departure or arrival airports, or travel dates; and then make your bid again with a higher price.

So the catch is to look at all the options of arrivals and departures and bid on the most popular airports, most convenient departure and arrival times first, and save some other airports in the same vicinity as a backup in case they do not accept your price.

Remember, once you make a bid and they accept it—there are no refunds or changes! So this system is only good if you have some flexibility in your schedule and know you won't need to make changes.

My friend Brenda Taylor had to drive fifty miles out of the way, leave on a date she didn't want to leave, and arrive later than expected just to save $50. Since she couldn't use the flight as a frequent-flier benefit on her usual airline, she decided it wasn't worth it. You'll have to decide if the savings are worth the inconveniences.

On the other hand, our oldest daughter, Missy, booked a flight from California to New York to see some friends for only $150. She booked it six months in advance, and it was truly worth the risk since inconvenience was a non-issue in her case.

Considering today's volatile world, if you're planning to fly outside the United States, you may want to look at *www.state.gov* for global travel restrictions before you book a flight.

Hotel

You can often find packages for great hotel rates at the airline Internet site when you book travel. You can also find great rates on car rentals when you're booking these other services. I've found that I'm getting an even better rate at the *www.southwestairlines.com* site on hotels and rentals than I would get bidding on a room or car at other travel sites. So when you're checking the airline fares from the previous paragraph, be sure to check the hotel and rental rates as well.

Besides some of the auction sites we've already mentioned, you can also check hotel sites for their weekly Internet specials. Try the following for e-mail alerts: Hyatt at *www.hyatt.com*, Radisson at *www.radisson.com/hotdeals*, the Holiday Inn at *www.basshotels.com/holiday-inn*, Best Western at *www.bestwestern.com*, and the Hilton at *www.hilton.com*.

> Try planning your vacations during off-seasons, if possible—you'll save significantly on everything from hotel rooms to area attractions.

Inexpensive Travel and Entertainment After the Honeymoon

Future Vacations: Plan Ahead

One of the reasons many couples overspend on vacations is because of a failure to plan ahead. They arrive at their destination and decide to take in several unplanned tourist attractions; they eat at specialty restaurants and buy overpriced souvenirs that will end up in next year's garage sale. This failure to plan ahead costs hundreds, if not thousands, of extra dollars each year.

Set a budget before you pull out of your driveway. Decide what activities take priority and *stay on budget*. Each spouse should contribute their ideas and decide on a plan that will accommodate as many interests as possible. For example, your hubby wants to go to the new Wet and Wild Water Park near your selected camping spot, but you want to go to the amusement park. The water park costs just as much as the amusement park, and you can't do both. Suggest a trip to the nearby beach on one day (since you have no beaches near your home) and a trip to the amusement park. Which, when discussed further, may satisfy your hubby. A good compromise, and you're still within budget.

Estimate the cost of meals, gas, and incidentals. Try planning your vacations during off-seasons, if possible—you'll save significantly on everything from hotel rooms to area attractions.

Select vacation areas in your locale. Since we move so much, we try to see everything there is to see within our area. We make "day trips" to area sites and save the cost of a hotel room. We pack our lunch and have a great time relaxing at a roadside picnic table.

Look for Last-Minute Deals

If you are planning another trip and are flexible in your schedule, take advantage of the last-minute deals offered by airlines and hotels. Moment's Notice is a booking specialist found at *www.moments-notice.com* or (718) 234–6295. They charge an annual fee of $25 but boast bargain-basement prices and some of the best values for cruises: Europe, Rio de Janeiro, and certain parts of the Caribbean. Sometimes if you buy a "Red-Eye Special" for substantial savings, you can show up at the ticket counter early and see if they can schedule you out on an earlier flight.

For last-minute hotel rooms, you could go to the very large TravelWeb site and look for Click-It Weekends! at *www.travelweb.com/TravelWeb/clickit.html.* Each Monday they post the coming weekend's special offers.

Have Fun

Some of the best dates I've had with Bob have been the simplest ones. When we take time out of a hectic schedule, turn off the radio, television, and computer, and just enjoy each other's company, we find we don't need much else!

Bob and I have discovered that we don't need a trip to Rio, an expensive meal at a posh restaurant, or a big day at a theme park to have genuine, guilt-free fun. Take it from me, and my mounds of correspondence with debt-ridden readers, paying a big credit card bill or accumulating debt is not fun.

Fun is about being together before the kids come along (or while they're asleep, if you already have children). It's learning to listen to the person you married and stay connected with the reasons why you love him or her. It's about learning to laugh at life's unexpected twists and turns.

Day Trips

It's been said that "change is as good as rest." So get out your map and look at day trips you can take. You may be surprised at how many fascinating little towns are within a short distance from your home. There will be lots of places you can enjoy going to look at historic buildings, architecture, and gardens or to wander around markets and antique stores.

Zoo Memberships

Most zoos are members of a reciprocal zoo association. This means you pay a fee with the zoo of your choice and you get reciprocal privileges in several hundred other zoos, aquariums, and wildlife parks across the country. Our local zoo in Alamogordo is a small facility and only charges $35 per year for a family membership. However, with our membership card we've gone to the El Paso zoo free (it would have cost $18 for the family for the day), the Albuquerque Biological park (saved $23 for the day), and the Los Angeles Zoo (saved $34). As a matter of fact, we maintained our zoo membership when we moved from New Mexico to New York and got to visit zoos in New York for less than the annual membership of our local zoo.

Check out the American Zoo Association at *www.aza.org*, where you can view the several hundred zoos available in this reciprocal zoo program. After we visited our friends Mark and Diane Thomas in Albuquerque, and they saw us get in free, they joined the Alameda Park Zoo in Alamogordo and had the membership tickets mailed to them in Albuquerque. Now they visit our zoo, their own zoo, and many others for a fraction of the price. These memberships can also offer discounts at the bookstore and passes to special exhibits.

For more information, you can contact our zoo at:

Alameda Park Zoo
PO Box 596
Alamogordo, NM 88310
(505) 439–4290
www.alamogordo.com/zoo.html

Museum Memberships

Museum memberships work the same way the zoo memberships do with a reciprocal list that can save you locally and when you travel. With our zoo and museum memberships, we are never at a loss for fun, free, and new things to do in another city. We joined the New Mexico Museum of Natural History for only $40 a year and received an ASTC (Association of Science Trade Centers) passport. This passport allowed us access to hundreds, even though we only visited a dozen other museums on our trips in the last year, *plus* our membership included passes to the Dynamax theater.

New Mexico Museum of Natural History
1801 Mountain Road NW
Albuquerque, NM
(505) 841–2803

You can search just about every museum in the country by area if you go to *archive.comblab.ox.ac.uk/other/museums/search.html*.

Something to remember: Museums participating in the ASTC Travel Passport Program agree to waive general admission fees for one another's members. Fees for planetariums, theaters, and special exhibitions are not waived unless specified.

With this pass we visit our local Space Museum, where the kids love to operate the new space shuttle simulator. Our friends joined this museum and sent an additional card to their college student daughter in New York City, so she can also have entertainment on a college student's budget. Check out the more than four hundred museums at *www.astc.org* for more information or write the museum listed above.

Dinner

Don't forget that there are coupons available for many dinner places you enjoy. Look in the free-standing inserts in your Sunday paper when you're collecting your grocery store coupons. Go to your favorite restaurant's site on the Internet by entering *www.* followed by your favorite restaurant's name and then *.com*. For example, check out *www.bennigans.com* and see what promotional offers they may have posted. Go to *www.valpak.com* for local offers and *www.citysearch.com* to find bargain restaurants neighborhood by neighborhood.

Maps

Whether you are taking a major cross-country trip, going to a nearby city, or just looking for that new restaurant across town, print out a free map from the Internet before you hit the road. Click on *www.mapquest.com* or *www.mapblast.com*, or for more specific road trips, try *www.mapsonus.com* and *www.interstate4U.com*.

The Travel Industry Association at *www.tia.org* lists state tourism offices with links and lots of pictures.

Weather

If you want to check out the weather where you're going, you can look at *www.weather.com*, *www.accuweather.com*, or *www.worldclimate.com*.

Redefine Entertainment

Life's simple pleasures *truly* are the best. Advertising tries to convince us that expensive entertainment is the ultimate. We feel compelled to work ourselves silly to afford that dream vacation to the Caribbean—then what? It's never enough. These "things" never truly satisfy until we can learn to enjoy and find our entertainment in the simple things. We can even find enjoyment in productivity.

The Library

The local library is a great source of entertainment. You can borrow videos, DVDs, books-on-tape, CDs, and audiocassettes, besides the ever-popular books. Many libraries offer free classes and guest lectures. Try researching your family tree at a library with a good genealogy reference section.

Games

Recently, it seems, families are rediscovering the lost art of game-playing. You know all those games you got as kids for Christmas and birthday presents? They're just taking up space on a shelf, when they could be a great source of entertainment and together time for the two of you. When surveys tell us the average amount of spouse-to-spouse time is measured in minutes, we know that game-playing isn't the only thing we may be missing in a marriage.

Sports and Exercise

Killing two birds with one stone is one of my favorite pastimes. Bob and I like to take a walk and talk at the same time. It accomplishes two important functions—exercise of the legs and the jaws. You and your husband might want to pick up a sport as a common recreation. Basketball, racquetball, skating, and jogging are all inexpensive and fun sports to participate in as a family. But doing something together like this is a great habit to start early on in your marriage.

Parks and Open Spaces

Few things are more romantic than a picnic in the park. If you have local public gardens or parks, make up a picnic lunch and soak in the scenery.

Hiking is also a great way to combine exercise with together time. Discover the countryside around you. You'll be amazed at what's on your doorstep. Search "Hiking Trails" on the Internet for a multitude of ideas. For a complete "what, when, where, and how" of hiking and walking, go to *http://dir.yahoo.com/Recreation/Outdoors/Hiking*, or for a full listing of national parks, go to *www.nps.gov/parks.html*. If you are a member of AAA, you must check out *www.aaa.com* for tried and true vacation sites. For state searches of hundreds of leisure activities on federal lands, go to *www.recreation.gov*.

Camping

We've saved the best for last. According to a recent survey, the most common denominator in individuals who expressed a satisfying childhood is camping. The least expensive way to camp is tent camping, and it's truly a family bonding experience. Camping saves money on hotel rooms and food. You may want to consider pooling your equipment with other couples to save expenses. For the novice, joining an experienced camping couple is a must. We learned so many helpful tips while camping with the Parker family at the annual July 4th weekend trip. We forgot the eggs, but they remembered them. We forgot the bait, but they had plenty. We forgot the baby-sitter, but Grandma Pauline was there. Camping can be a great, relaxing time!

> **The most common denominator in individuals who expressed a satisfying childhood is camping.**

Camping equipment can be found at garage sales and thrift shops. Make sure the items work and all the parts are there. Before you take the big plunge and buy a camper, tent trailer, or motor home, consider renting a camper for a weekend. When buying a camper unit, consider your budget and available money for such a purchase—but you just might consider it an investment in your marriage.

There's an old saying: "The family that plays together, stays together." This is an especially good habit to get firmly established in your marriage *now*, before your family begins to expand. It's important that you begin the concept of regular rest and relaxation with the honeymoon and continue it all the way to the golden anniversary. Your lives will be fuller, your bodies healthier, and your spirits will fly higher.

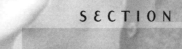
King of the Castle
and Queen of Hearts

Building Your Relationship

CHAPTER 4

ALAS, MY LOVE! I HAVE FOUND YOU!

We're Back From the Honeymoon, Now What?

We got back from our honeymoon on a Friday. By that Sunday I realized that I had married a man with a problem.

I had no idea.

I was shocked.

I was embarrassed.

It was then I knew ... this was war! A tug of war, to be precise.

When the Sunday paper arrived, Bob ran outside to retrieve it and brought it back to our front porch with a slightly half-witted expression on his face. That should have been my first hint, but I remained clueless. After all, he was my Prince Charming, my Knight Upon a White Steed. How could he possibly have ... a flaw?!

My picture-perfect image of Bob began to change as soon as I asked to see the morning paper before he had opened it. He looked at me incredulously, as if I had just asked him if we could dedicate our first-born to Baal. He then responded with the maturity of a three-year-old: "I had it first!"

I was surprised by his reaction, but I nonchalantly reached for the paper and held my ground.

"All I want are the coupons and *Parade* magazine," I explained calmly.

He quickly jerked it out of my hand, "I *said*, I had it *first!*"

Okay, I thought, *no more Mrs. Nice Newlywed!*

I was quick.

I grabbed the paper and quickly tried to walk away.

I was jerked back and found myself face-to-face with Bob the Newspaper Hog.

I wanted the coupons and *he*, well, he wanted—*gasp!* the *comics!*

He pulled and I jerked. He pulled again and I *called* him a jerk.

Tempers flared.

We couldn't seem to get a grip on ourselves *or* the paper, and the plastic bag encasing the morning treasure finally gave way. The paper spilled into ten directions onto the front porch. Bob scrambled for his precious comics, while I scrambled for the coupon inserts. But the *real* trouble had only just begun.

Bob began to read the comics, right there on the front porch. His guffaws were not exactly quiet and demure like most self-respecting men. They were loud. They sounded like the mating call of a great Canadian moose. I felt like I was at the zoo. Frankly, I would have given anything to be at the zoo rather than on the porch with this cackling weirdo. His bellowing brought the *neighbors* out of their homes to see what animal had been let loose in the apartment complex. I thought they'd see the slightly eccentric pilot laughing at the Sunday comics and go back into their homes. But no! They pulled up chairs for the gathering crowd. One industrious kid even sold coffee and donuts for twenty-five cents each!

It was then that I realized the honeymoon was over.

When Bob finished the *Wizard of Id*, the final comic strip in the section, he finally stopped his bellowing, and it was only then that he realized he'd drawn a crowd. With the sideshow over, everyone folded up their lawn chairs and went back into their apartments. But not before Bob bought a donut (that's yet *another* addiction, but let's handle one at a time).

When I got over the shock of it all and confronted Bob with his embarrassing guffawing "problem," his explanation was simple: "It takes so little to keep an idiot happy."

There tends to be some moment of truth for all couples that happens during or after the honeymoon, when they realize their lives have dramatically changed forever. With me, it was the comic experience, one that I desperately tried to change in Bob, but a habit that he continues to this day. The kids pull up chairs, make microwave popcorn, and are entertained for about fifteen minutes each Sunday morning, listening to their father honk like an injured goose. (Which is the *real* reason we're perpetually late for church.)

For Bob, the moment of truth was when he noticed that I squeezed the toothpaste tube from the middle rather than the end and put the toilet paper on the holder *the wrong way*. For my sister-in-law, Debby, it was the first time she had to do laundry for her husband and handle his dirty underwear. For my friend Martha, it was the first time she got sick and still had to make dinner because her husband was on a tight schedule that didn't allow for sick new brides.

For others, it will be the first time they have to sit down and pay bills, realizing that they still have more month left at the end of the paycheck. There are positive realizations mixed in as well. It might be the first holiday you share together when you realize that you and your husband are now a family. Or the first time you give your name as *Mrs.* So-and-So or tell your co-workers that *your husband* gave you that string of pearls for your wedding gift. It's a special and a scary feeling all at the same time. But at some point we all realize that the wedding festivities are over, and a new life has begun—for better or for worse!

So where do you start? What do you do now that the honeymoon is over? What's next? This chapter and, indeed, the rest of this book, are going to address some basic "housekeeping" and relational issues that every new bride needs to understand in order to make her home a castle fit for the king and queen.

Housekeeping—Organizing Your New Home

One of the most formidable tasks after the honeymoon lies in getting your home (and yourselves) organized. Here's a basic checklist of tasks you might want to complete during the first month of marriage as well as organizational tips for a variety of household items:

Delegating Tasks—Deciding Who Does What

There are a lot of details to take care of in the first month—and every month—of marriage. Who's going to make sure the thank-you notes get written, the taxes filed? Who's going to add both names to the titles, your rings to the homeowner's policy, your spouse to the medical plan (if needed)? Is he going to pay the bills, or are you? Who's going to do the laundry, take out the garbage, and make sure there's milk in the fridge and the recycling gets to the curb?

> Thank-you notes should be written and mailed within a month of your return from your honeymoon, so make them a priority on your to-do list.

To make sure nothing essential falls through the cracks—and to keep conflicts at a minimum—make a checklist of everything that needs to get done in your home on a monthly basis and who is going to do each task. Work on this together; it's a little too soon in your marriage for "honey do" lists!

Thank You, Thank You, Thank You!

I've heard one too many brides gripe and complain about "writing those thank-you notes" as if it were a colossal chore equivalent to the building of the Great Pyramids. Writing thank-you notes is a privilege because it means that you were *gifted* by someone. It's one less thing you'll have to buy. For five minutes "labor" of writing a note and the price of a postage stamp, you received an item of real value. Where else can you "work" for a few minutes and get a place setting of china? How long do you have to work at your job to earn enough to buy a toaster? By changing your perspective on these notes, you can breeze through them with genuine gratitude. Thank-you notes should be written and mailed within a month of your return from your honeymoon, so make them a priority on your to-do list. I'd recommend that your husband write the wedding gift thank-yous to his friends and family, since he knows them better and would add a more personal touch. It is the bride's responsibility, however, to write the thank-you notes for her shower, her family, and her friends.

As you write, remember the three ABCs of writing a good thank-you note:

1. *Accuracy.* Address it to the people by name (i.e., "Dear Tom and Alice" or "Dear Dr. and Mrs. Thomas") and be sure to include your spouse, such as "Tom and I thank you . . ."
2. *Brevity.* You don't have to write two-page notes to each person, except perhaps your parents or someone else who went above and beyond to help in your wedding planning. A few sincere sentences will suffice.
3. *Clarity.* Be sure to mention the item they gave you (i.e., "Thank you for the generous check" or "Thank you for the knitted poodle Kleenex box holder").

Mail

You may be amazed at how many mailing lists newlyweds end up on and how much mail you and your new hubby will receive. Here are tips to manage it before you're buried under it! Practice the four D's:

> *Do* it now (pay the bill, respond to the letter).
> *Delegate* (let your hubby take care of it).
> *Delay* it (put it in the bill drawer or project file for later).
> *Dump* it (into the trash—especially catalogs or other temptations to overspend).

Closets—Six Steps to More Space

Step 1: *Starting*

You are going to need to get an accurate picture of what items you need to store and what kind of space you have to store them in. Start by taking *everything* out of your closet and then take some measurements. Write the dimensions of your closet on a piece of paper. Then realize that you've got some ruthless decisions to make.

Step 2: *Sorting*

Start by sorting your clothes into basic groups: shirts, skirts, coats and jackets, etc. Once you've got your wardrobe organized, divide each group into three more piles: (1) put away;

(2) give away; and (3) throw away. To help with the decisions you must make about these clothes, ask yourself what professional "clutter busters" ask: Does it fit? Is it out of date? What shape is it in? When was the last time I wore it? If it has been over a year, it is highly unlikely you will ever wear it again—despite your best intentions. Toss it!

Now is also the time to get hubby to go through the same process with his clothes, especially if you'll be sharing a closet. This is your opportunity to encourage him to consider donating that muscle shirt from high school or that "lucky" fishing shirt.

Step 3: Salvage

Take all the items you have in your "put away" pile and look them over closely. You'll need to either wash it, clean it, fix it, or put it away. If you've been meaning to reattach the straps on that cocktail dress,.get the spot out of that tank top, sew a button on that sweater coat, and fix the hem on those trousers—now's the time. Send your discards to the local thrift shop, consign the nicer items, or give them to someone who might truly need them.

Step 4: Space and Sweep

Now it's time to plan your space. Start fresh by sweeping, dusting, wiping shelves and rods. Remove nails and hooks that could tear or snag garments. With an empty, clean space at your disposal, check out what additions you'll want to make to your closet. If you need more room, look up. It's easier than you think to add high shelving—perfect for seasonal items like winter sweaters and summer hats. This may be out-of-reach storage, so consider picking up a folding step stool and adding a light to your closet as well.

Step 5: Some Assembly Required

You'll need proper hangers for your closets: that means getting rid of all those dry cleaner freebies. Hang every item on a separate hanger, and keep in mind, your clothes will keep their shape oh-so-much-better if stored properly. Put pants on pant hangers, skirts on skirt hangers, and delicates on fabric-covered hangers. Take down items that may droop or stretch on hangers and store these folded on shelves or in drawers instead.

Step 6: Storage

Store your better clothing in fabric garment bags, not in plastic hanging bags or dry cleaners' plastic covers. Over time chemicals trapped in plastic can harm and discolor your clothing. If you want to preserve your wedding gown, have it professionally cleaned and boxed for storage. As you reassemble your closet, keep similar items together, arranged by level of formality or by season. If you live in an extreme climate, group items by season, then by type, then by level of formality. That way when summer rolls around, you can simply rearrange your closet so that winter items are in the back and summer items are within easy reach. Now that you're organized, it will be easier to keep it that way if you keep it up daily!

Kitchen Organization

Logical and Convenient Organize your kitchen in a way that will make it easy to find the tool or dish you need. Coffee cups, coffee filters, and coffee should be in the cabinet above the coffeemaker. Cooking pots and pans, as well as hot pads, kitchen towels, and oven mitts, should be near the stove. Plates should be in one cabinet, while cups and glasses of all kinds are stored in another. Silverware could be in a drawer beneath these cabinets for more efficient table setting. Buy a flatware organizer that has places for knives, spoons, and forks.

One Junk Drawer Is Enough Avoid mass clutter of kitchen gadgets by purchasing sorters for your kitchen drawers or a countertop organizer. Beware of the temptation to get too many junk drawers going. One drawer with all the odds and ends should be enough.

Add-On's If you want to make your new husband happy, suggest a trip to Home Depot! Look at their kitchen organization section. Sometimes drawers that slide out, lazy Susans for the corner of the kitchen, or under-the-counter recycling bins can transform an average kitchen into a super-organized kitchen.

Ring Thing Either hang a decorative hook by the kitchen sink or get a special ceramic ring box to stow your watch and ring while you work in the kitchen.

Put a Cork in It If your cabinet design allows, glue a twelve-inch square of thin cork to the inside of the cabinet nearest your counter work area. Tack the recipe you're working on within eye range for easy access and avoiding mistakes (like substituting baking powder for flour as I once did!).

Phone Home! Invest in a cordless phone if you don't already have one. This one item can save tons of time in the kitchen. While you talk you can continue to make dinner, unload the dishwasher, set the table, or organize a drawer.

Paper Work

You may wonder how long you should keep paper work. Here's a basic list:

Six Years
> bank statements
> canceled checks
> investment records

Until Updated
> contracts
> credit card account numbers
> car, home insurance
> loan agreements
> will

Until Sale
> home purchase and improvement records
> real estate deeds
> receipts for large purchases
> service contracts and warranties
> vehicle titles

Forever
> birth or adoption certificates
> marriage certificate
> military records
> life insurance policies
> Social Security card
> tax returns
> your spouse

Heart-Keeping: Building Your Relationship

Now that we've got the house under control, let's move on to something even more important—reining in our expectations of developing a flawless relationship with our spouse so that we can work on a realistic one.

The Phantom Menace

Before we go any further and begin to talk about things you "should" and "should not" do in a marriage, now is a very good time to take inventory of the expectations we bring to marriage. In their book *Building Your Mate's Self-Esteem,* Dennis and Barbara Rainey refer to a phenomenon in marriages called *phantoms.*

For a number of years Bob taught young men to fly the F–4 Phantom. Thirty years ago the Phantom was *the* technological wonder. It flew in low and fast. Bombs were dropped before the enemy knew the aircraft was in the area. Thus the name "Phantom" was given to that airplane.

The Raineys defined a phantom as:

> An unattainable mental image or standard by which we measure our performance, abilities, looks, character, and life. It is perfect, idyllic. A phantom, by definition, is an illusion, an apparition, or a resemblance of reality (Thomas Nelson, 1995, 34).

All of us have phantoms—mental images of what we believe we should be—and they can become a real menace if we let them take over. So right now, why not take the time to think about *your* phantom. Take it a step further and write it down. To get you started, I'll share the phantom list I wrote several years ago:

Top Twenty Phantoms: Ellie's Phantom

- My phantom is 5'8" tall, a perfect size 8, and never has a bad hair day.
- She runs five miles daily. As a matter-of-fact, she's in training for the Pikes Peak Ascent run, which is a thirteen-mile run up a 14,000-foot mountain.
- She makes all her baby, wedding, birthday, hospitality, and Christmas gifts by hand.
- She sends thirty letters to friends and family every month.
- She recycles newspapers, aluminum cans, cardboard, plastic, and glass, as well—not due to financial necessity but because of her concern for the environment.
- Of course she is an exceptional wife and mother who is *always* in a cheerful mood when her husband comes home from work. Even when he's late for dinner and the pot roast looks more like beef jerky and the kids have been candidates for the Mischief Hall of Fame.
- She is never irritable or short-tempered with the children.
- When administering discipline, she *always* takes Dr. Dobson's advice, making sure to balance the scales of love and justice.
- She obeys all traffic rules and never speeds, even on the rare occasion when she is late for an appointment.
- She is patient and understanding with the idiots who try to run her off the road.
- She never over-commits herself socially, in her work, or in her daily schedule.
- She volunteers often and manages to fulfill *every* exciting opportunity that comes her way.
- She cooks a well-balanced meal *each* night, keeps an immaculate home, and makes her own flour, bread, cookies, cakes, and pasta.
- She homeschools her children and is a gracious hostess socially at her husband's formal functions.

- She writes well and meets her deadlines.
- She speaks with confidence in front of an audience that doesn't get her jokes.
- The latest styles are never lost on this woman.
- She is kind to the unkind.
- She takes time out for friends who need her.
- She *never* puts her foot in her mouth.

The important thing to remember is that we cannot do it all—at least not all at the same time. Go back and look at your list and mark each one with an "R" for realistic or a "U" for unrealistic. Then build your priorities and expectations based on those items that are realistic for you personally and get rid of the phantom menace.

Success

You know the saying: People don't plan to fail, they just fail to plan. According to Sally Ride, a successful astronaut who has accomplished more in her life so far than most, there are three secrets to success:

1. Be willing to learn new things.
2. Be able to assimilate new information quickly.
3. Be able to get along with and work with other people.

Sounds pretty simple, huh? But this kind of an approach to life requires focus and diligence. It requires a plan. Let's take Sally's philosophy and apply it to marriage in general and also specifically to the other information you'll be learning in this book.

1. *Be willing to learn new things.*

The sooner a bride realizes that she doesn't know everything about married life and that she needs help, the better off she'll be. This may mean you learn a new dish to cook that your spouse loves (and you may not love). It also applies to learning better and more effective ways to communicate, organize your finances, and appreciate male/female differences.

I have been privileged to be a mentor to and be mentored by many women throughout my life, and there's one and only one thing that will cause me to terminate the relationship—an unteachable spirit. As long as a woman keeps her heart open and teachable, there is hope. The day you believe you have nothing more to learn is the day you begin to shrink on the inside into oblivion and irrelevance. Be willing to learn and you can impact the world.

> The sooner a bride realizes that she doesn't know everything about married life and that she needs help, the better off she'll be.

2. *Be able to assimilate new information quickly.*

Isn't this a natural trait rather than a learned response? Not really. Sure, there are people who seem to have photographic memories and can reconstruct a conversation or other information almost perfectly. But there's more to this point than an ability to regurgitate information. It means that when we are presented with new information, we become critical thinkers. This requires effort, and if you're used to spending a lot of time in front of the TV, computer games, or other electronic stimulation, you begin to lose your ability to think on your own and think well. So perhaps a good start would be to minimize how much television you watch and other "non-thinking" stimuli.

Then as you read, for example, the chapter on male/female differences, you begin to think about how you fit the description. You can better understand that your husband is not *better or worse*—but *different,* and how it could impact your relationship. Soak in all the information you can and let it be released in practical ways that help you grow as a person.

3. *Be able to get along with and work with other people.*

Let's face it. Some people are "upfront" folks that just love to be around people. But even if you're not a people person in the traditional sense, you can still learn to get along with and work well with other people. It's essential if you are to have success in your marriage, work, and other relationships. There's a Scripture that says, "As long as it lies within you, live at peace with all men." This means that you cannot control other people—what they say, how they respond, and what they do. But you *can* control your response.

So if we carry that thought to its logical conclusion, we won't be able to say, "They *made* me mad." Because no one *forces* you to become angry. We'd have to say, "I *chose* to get mad over what that toad did." Getting along well with other people means we take responsibility for our thoughts, words, and actions. You will rarely find people who work well with other people going around blaming others for the things that happen in their own lives. This means that when something rubs us the wrong way about someone else, the higher road is to build a bridge and get over it. Now, how's that for a string of clichés?

If You Had It to Do Over Again

There is a favorite line of mine from the book *Anne of Avonlea* by L. M. Montgomery, where Anne has gotten into yet another one of her scrapes. She says, "Tomorrow is always fresh, with no mistakes in it!"

One day as Anne and her guardian, Marilla, are walking down the tree-lined road home, Anne is caught in her seemingly endless pastime of daydreaming.

Exasperated, Marilla looks at Anne: "When are you going to stop all these endless imaginations? You do go on so!"

Undaunted, Anne matches her steps to Marilla's. "But Marilla, didn't you ever *imagine* things were different than they are?"

The older woman's firm reply is a simple "No!"

Anne looks into the distance dreamily with a wistful tone and laments, "Oh, Marilla! How *much* you miss!"

This series of books was written over fifty years ago, but the wisdom found in this fiction applies to where you are right now. Your today, tomorrow, is fresh—there are no mistakes in it. Yes, from time to time you'll fail in your marriage—that's life. There will be words you wish you could take back, but you can't. There may be accidents, circumstances beyond your control, or an assortment of unimagined challenges. But as one who is just starting out, NOW is a good time to imagine the kind of life you'd like to look back on one day. Imagination is a wonderful gift from God, and it can be used in a good and healthy way if we choose to let it play that kind of a supportive role.

The following was written by an unknown author, and I sometimes think I know why he may have chosen to remain anonymous. This piece was found in *Lists to Live By* (Multnomah, 1999), a compilation by Alice Gray, Steve Stephans, and John Van Diest. As you read it, think about what you'd like to remember when you look back on today and your future tomorrows.

If I Had It to Do Over Again

I would love my wife more in front of my children.

I would laugh with my children more—at our mistakes and our joys.

I would listen more—even to the youngest child.

I would be more honest about my own weakness and stop pretending perfection.

I would pray differently for my family.

I would pay more attention to little things, deeds, and words of love and kindness.

Finally, if I had it to do all over again, I would share God more intimately with my family. I would use ordinary things that happened in every ordinary day to point them to God.

CHAPTER 5

IF YOU *REALLY* LOVED ME, YOU COULD READ MY MIND

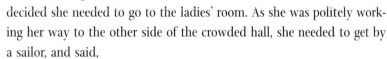

Communication With a Different Species

My mom was a military bride who married a sailor in the Navy and came to the United States from Spain to make a new life in a different culture. She knew very little English when she first came to America, and her accent was quite thick. A week after they arrived in this new country my mom found herself at a formal military ball with my father, who looked dashing in his uniform. She was embarrassed by the fact that she didn't know very much English, so my dad said that in order to learn the language she should "*Mingle* with people; just walk around and *mingle*."

He went to get them some Cokes while she stood in the same place for several minutes wondering what in the world "mingle" meant. She looked around at the sea of faces and decided she needed to go to the ladies' room. As she was politely working her way to the other side of the crowded hall, she needed to get by a sailor, and said,

"Eh, kiss me!"

He stared at her, looking a bit baffled, to which she repeated herself firmly and politely,

"Eh, kiss me!"

So he did.

She was shocked, and reacted by slapping him across the face.

Paquita's husband quickly came to her side and explained to the sailor, who was still rubbing his stinging cheek, "Uh, she doesn't know English very well, and she thought she was saying, 'Excuse me.' "

That first year was only the beginning of a steady stream of change. My mom not only learned a new language and culture but she also moved from Indiana to Texas to California, and had three children and nine grandchildren along the way.

My mom isn't alone in this business of change. All human beings have to face changes that shake us out of our comfort zones and force us to accept new norms. These adjustments, in one form or another, continue throughout our lives.

As a new bride, one of the things you will need to learn about is the language of love and that "foreign-sounding language" your husband will sometimes speak. For example, studies indicate that a man needs to speak about 25,000 words a day to feel validated, while a woman needs to speak 50,000! The problem is that most men have spoken 24,990 words by the time they get home from work and all they have left is one "yeah," a "not much," a couple of "nothings," three "no's," and maybe a grunt or two. This may be as foreign to some brides as Texan-speak is to Californian-speak, but the language your husband speaks *can* be learned with a few simple lessons.

Male/Female Differences

For the last two decades our society has wasted a lot of brain cells pretending that men and women are the same. This dynamic can be very damaging to communication. Believing in equal pay for equal work isn't the same as believing I can bench-press 200 pounds like my husband can. Being different isn't bad! Bob ain't never gonna have babies, and I (hopefully) will never have to shave a beard. We're simply different—but as the French say, *"Vive la différence!"*

In case you're not entirely convinced, here's a quick rundown on just one of the physical differences between men and women—the brain. According to a March 6, 2002, report on *brainplace.com*:

Cell numbers   Men have 4 percent more brain cells than women, and about 100 grams more of brain tissue. Many women have asked why men need more brain tissue in order to get the same things done.

Right brain/left brain   Even though men have more brain cells, it is reported that women have more connections between brain cells. Since women have more connections between the right and left sides of their brain, they tend to be more verbal, relationally oriented, and can accomplish many things at once. Since men primarily draw from the left side of their brain, they are not as verbal, tend to be fact-oriented, and can't watch the kids and read the paper at the same time.

Language   For men, language is most often just in the dominant hemisphere (usually the left side), but a larger number of women seem to be able to use both sides for language. This gives them a distinct advantage. If a woman has a stroke in the left front side of the brain, she may still retain some language from the right front side. Men who have the same left-sided damage are less likely to recover as fully.

Limbic size   This has to do with bonding/nesting instincts. Current research has demonstrated that females, on average, have a larger deep limbic system than males. This gives females several advantages. Due to the larger deep limbic brain, women are more in touch with their feelings; they are generally better able to express their feelings than men.

Bonding   Women have a greater ability to bond and to be connected to others (which is why women are the primary caretakers for children—there is no society on earth where men are primary caretakers for children). However, having this larger deep limbic system leaves a female somewhat more susceptible to depression, especially at times of significant hormonal changes, such as the onset of puberty, before menses, after the birth of a child, and at menopause.

He Says/She Means

One of the best books on male/female differences was written by my friends Bill and Pam Farrel entitled *Men Are Like Waffles—Women Are Like Spaghetti* (Harvest House, 2001). I heard Pam give the following speech to a room full of women, and they were dying laughing. Enjoy:

If She Says	She Really Means
We need.	I want.
It's your decision.	The correct decision should be obvious.
Do what you want.	You'll pay for this later.
You're . . . so manly.	You need a shave and you sweat a lot.
This kitchen is so inconvenient.	I want a new house.
You have to learn to communicate.	Just agree with me.
I'm sorry.	You'll be sorry.
You're certainly attentive tonight.	Is sex all you ever think about?

If He Says	He Really Means
I'm hungry.	I'm hungry.
I'm sleepy.	I'm sleepy.
I'm tired.	I'm tired.
Do you want to go to a movie?	I'd eventually like to have sex with you.
Can I take you out to dinner?	I'd eventually like to have sex with you.
What's wrong? (first time)	I don't see why you're making such a big deal about this.
What's wrong? (second time)	What meaningless, self-inflicted psychological trauma are you going through now?
What's wrong? (third time)	I guess sex tonight is out of the question?

The point of this section is that men tend to say what they really mean, but women often say one thing and mean something entirely different. We expect our guys to read our minds and be more intuitive than their left-brain dominance allows them to be. The lesson is that we need to be more specific on what our needs and wants are, and we need to take our men at face value (except when it comes to their agenda on having sex). Speaking of sex, the next section will discuss the primary needs a man has and the answer may not be what you think it is.

Three Basic Needs of a Man

Knowing your husband's basic needs (as well as your own) creates a greater sense of understanding toward your mate. If you understand him and learn to appreciate him for the way he was created, if you can learn what makes him tick and what makes him explode, then this understanding can minimize conflict and lead to greater mutual fulfillment in your marriage. So let's look at a man's basic needs.

Basic Need #1—Sexual Fulfillment

According to Dr. Kevin Leman's excellent book *Sex Begins in the Kitchen* (Revell, 1999, 149):

> "What's the #1 need for a man in marriage?
> Affirmation? It's important, but not the top need.
> Communication? Get real! Sex? Now you're talking ... but this isn't exactly right either.
> Most women think that most men are 'after only one thing' but that's far too simplistic. **The #1 need is not sex but sexual fulfillment.**"

The reason we women tend to get the two confused is that we don't see the difference between sex and sexual fulfillment. We'll look at this in greater depth in our next chapter on intimacy, but at this point, we need to realize that a man's sexual need is far more than just the physical. It is mental and emotional. These latter two aspects of sexual fulfillment are directly related to communication, and we'll also get to that important topic later in this chapter.

Basic Need #2—Respect

Rodney Dangerfield has become famous for his one-liners about how "I can't get no respect." His wife seems to be the primary target of many of these "lack of respect" jokes. For example, Rodney says, "I call my wife to tell her I got hit by a bus on the way home from work, and she says, 'I guess this means I'll have to walk the dog.'"

A man's sexual need is far more than just the physical. It is mental and emotional.

Men don't seem to just *want* respect from their brides, they actually *need* it to feel they are important and that what they do matters. This isn't the same as feeding a man's ego. We are talking about genuine praise for actions, attitudes, and characteristics that you admire in your man. *Tell him* about things you appreciate. This also means that when the women at a Christmas party start to slam their man verbally and publicly, you refrain.

Bob and I made a commitment to each other the first month we were married: We would never make a joke at the other's expense either in public or private. It's been hard to keep that commitment, especially among fighter pilots who delight in making themselves feel important by cutting the other guy down. One of their favorite lines was "You are so pretty, how did you get stuck with a guy like Bob?" Then they would laugh at their wit and be very pleased with themselves. If I laughed and said nothing, it would seem as if I agreed. So I would say, "Are you kidding? I got the better end of this deal—I married the 'World's Greatest Fighter Pilot!'" Not only did it shut those guys up, it gave me my favorite saying that I still use today.

Basic Need #3—To Be Needed

This final "top three" need is directly related to the first two. A husband's sexual fulfillment is physical, emotional, and mental. When he feels that he is sexually satisfying his wife, giving her what she really wants and needs, then he feels good. When she respects him for who he is and what he does for her, then it naturally makes him feel needed. All three of these needs are interrelated and fit together tightly.

Showing your husband that you need him *doesn't* mean you turn into some helpless damsel in distress every time you can't reach a can off the top shelf! It *does* mean that you let him know what your needs are: emotionally, physically, sexually, spiritually, and mentally. Whenever he meets those needs, let him know, specifically, how much you appreciate him. He can do the same for you. It's a great way to live—seeing which one can "out compliment" the other.

Her Three Basic Needs

Two decades ago, when Ann Landers surveyed her female readers about women's basic needs, millions of readers were shocked to discover that a surprising number of women could live without sex if they just had affection.

Basic Need #1—Affection

The respondents to the survey indicated that hugs, kisses, holding hands, and back rubs were more important than sex. This is going to be a major revelation to men when they hear it for the first time, because they are wired soooo differently than women, but it's true. Women need to be touched, stroked, embraced—for affection, not just foreplay. If Bob gives me a tender hug, hoping it will lead to sex, then it doesn't communicate to me that he loves me—it just makes me feel he's using affection to get sex. But if he periodically hugs me for no reason, or holds my hand just because he's near, then that meets my #1 basic need and makes me feel truly loved.

Basic Need(s) #2—Honesty, Openness, Conversation

Because women are so well-connected between both hemispheres of their brain, they tend to be a little more complicated in their needs orientation. Therefore, our basic need #2 is actually a group of closely related needs that connect to the verbal and emotional sides of our brain. The problem is that men tend to focus on facts and may even grunt instead of talking.

"How was your day, dear?"

"Hurrmp!"

> "Wives need to understand their husbands' lack of communication, but they don't have to settle for it."

We quoted Dr. Kevin Leman under the "Three Basic Needs of Man." Dr. Leman goes on to say, "Wives need to understand their husbands' lack of communication, but they don't have to settle for it." We just need to pick the optimum timing to get their conversation going down the right track. I've learned to give Bob time and space to wind down from his workday, and he does the same for me when I've come back from a speaking trip. While I *appreciate* this transition period, Bob seems to *need* it before I can draw out the best in conversation from him.

Some husbands try to articulate how they feel about an issue, but many guys are as likely to express their feelings as they are to know where the measuring cups are kept. Sure, there are guys who bake better than their wives (and blessed is the woman who finds one of these), but most guys don't cook any better than they communicate. But they can learn. And by learning how to meet their wife's needs, they end up being needed, which leads them to sexual fulfillment, which makes for a nice circle of love where his needs and her needs are mutually met and mastered.

Basic Need #3—Commitment to Family/Finances

"Unfortunately," says Dr. Leman, "many men still pursue the role of the uninvolved bread-winner. They work eighty hours a week to make good money so they can buy a spiffy house in an upscale neighborhood—but they never see the family that lives there!" While working hard seems to address these last two needs together, it can also frequently get out of balance. Most women say they need financial security but few will sacrifice commitment to the family in order to gain this kind of security.

By working through the financial chapters later in this book, you and your husband will actually be meeting this need for financial commitment, and by managing your finances well, you lessen the likelihood that you or your husband will have to work a second job to make ends meet. This, in turn, helps your husband have the time to be more committed to the marital relationship and your family—whether it consists of two members or ten!

Communication: Key to Your Marriage

Norman Wright wrote an excellent book that has helped Bob and me significantly, and I'd highly recommend it: *Communication: Key to Your Marriage* (Regal Books, revised 2000). What I appreciate most about this book is its practicality; it gives specific examples of how communication is supposed to work, how to reduce marital conflict, manage anger, build one another's self-esteem, and just plain listen to each other.

Three Basic Principles of Effective Communication

Principle #1—Active Listening Stephen R. Covey, the *New York Times* bestselling author, said in *Seven Habits of Highly Effective Families* (Golden Books, 1997, 237) that listening means "Seek first to understand before being understood." When it comes to communication, we are all products of our experience, childhood, values, assumptions, and expectations. Covey went on to say, "At the heart of every family pain is misunderstanding." The point is: if we want to be heard by our spouse, we must first seek to hear what he/she is *really* saying. Not what we think they are saying.

One time Bob came home from a long day of work and I met him at the door. I'd had a long day with three preschoolers who seemed intent on setting the record for how many messes they could make in one day. I had cleaned spilled sugar, dirty diapers, smushed bananas, and cracker crumbs all day long.

"The house is a mess!" Bob said as he walked in the door.

My first inclination was to deck him. But thankfully I'd just read Covey's book and thought I'd try the "paraphrasing" exercise he recommended.

"Oh, *dearest,* what do you mean when you say 'the house is a mess'? Do you mean that you think I haven't cleaned it to your standards?" I asked.

Bob shook his head emphatically, "*No,* I don't mean the *inside* of the house, I mean the *outside*. I should have cut the grass last Saturday, and it's gotten out of control. I need to mow it!"

> If we want to be heard by our spouse, we must first seek to hear what he/she is *really* saying.

By repeating or paraphrasing what you *thought* you heard your spouse say, you learn what they *really* meant to say, and you become an active listener.

Principle #2—Use "I" Messages Rather Than "You" When we have understood our partner and we are trying to get them to understand our perspective, it is important to use "I" messages. Rather than a lengthy explanation, let's just look at an example:

Tom: Why are you so angry over something so small?

Angie: Because you never listen to me!

Tom: Okay, so it's my fault that you're going ballistic over something so stupid as taking out the trash. Great!

Angie: Oh, you're just like my father. You never do anything around this house!

Tom and Angie obviously need a Communication 101 course because their discourse is getting nowhere. But if they try to speak in "I" messages about how they feel and their perspective, then their conversation loses the accusatory tone that "you" messages tend to send. See how it works:

Tom: Why are you so angry over something so small?

Angie: Because I feel that I'm not being heard and that's not a small thing to me.

Tom: But I just forgot to take out the trash; that doesn't mean I'm not listening to you.

Angie: I grew up with a father who was like Archie Bunker, and my mom was constantly scrambling around the house doing all the work. I'm afraid that by constantly forgetting the work you agreed to, I may end up being just like my mom—carrying the lion's share of the work around the house.

Tom: But I'm not like your dad and I don't have any intention of not doing my part. Keeping our home nice is important to me, and I'm sorry if you feel I wasn't listening. I'll take out the trash right now (*and maybe we can have sex later,* Tom thinks to himself).

You can see how the irritation escalated in the first example and how it was minimized in the second. When Angie focused on her perspective and feelings rather than Tom's shortcomings and faults, there was a much greater chance of true understanding. That is the benefit of using "I" messages.

> **You and your mate won't always see eye to eye, but you *can* decide upfront how conflicts will be resolved.**

Principle #3—Agree to Healthy Resolutions   There are four basic resolutions to conflict: (1) A win/lose where someone wins at someone else's expense; (2) a lose/lose where no one wins; (3) a win/win where both partners win; and (4) an "agreement to disagree."

I will never forget a time in my advanced studies in college when we had a communication exercise in our small group. I was elected the spokesperson, and we had a mock negotiation phase where we could decide the outcome. Instead of going for a healthy resolution, I tricked the spokesperson from the other group and gained a win/lose in favor of our team. It humiliated the other person, and he blew up in front of the class, yelled, and left the room. I felt terrible, and I learned a valuable lesson about negotiations: when you win at someone else's expense, it doesn't feel as good as you thought it would. I ended up apologizing publicly to my teammates and the other spokesperson. It took the rest of the semester to regain my credibility with my class, and I don't think I ever regained my previous position of respect with the other spokesperson.

You and your mate won't always see eye to eye, but you *can* decide upfront how conflicts will be resolved. Agree, early in your marriage, to either go for the win/win solution or the decision to agree to disagree.

Bonus Tip: Ask Forgiveness and Freely Give It

Today the father of one of my son's friends, Danny, caught up with me in the school parking lot to tell me something that happened with our youngest son, seven-year-old Joshua. Danny walked into the boy's bathroom and found Joshua and his friend Zack standing in the corner, talking and giggling.

Danny asked, "What are you guys doing?"

To which Joshua smiled mischievously. "We're thinking of names to call a girl in our class. Silly names. We don't like her."

Danny looked stern, "Hey! That's not very nice to call little girls names. Aren't you one of the Kay boys? I know your parents!"

Knowing he was caught, Joshua reacted faster than a quick-change artist, "Uh, did I say we were *making up* names? Actually, we were talking about the name of a *poor family*. Uh . . . a poor family in our church, and how we need to collect some food to give to them!"

All Danny could say was "Yeah, you're one of those Kay kids all right!"

We all make mistakes in marriage. Just like Joshua, we sometimes get caught and may even lie. We grouse and pretend we're hormonal. We get angry, yell, and then feel terrible. (One note on anger: If you or your spouse is having a significant and repeated problem with anger, ask for professional help. When it comes to taking care of issues like these—earlier is better than later but later is better than never.)

The point *is not*: we need to try to be perfect. The point is: we're *not* perfect but we can be forgiven. There's a Scripture verse that says, "Never let the sun go down on your anger." It's a good principle to live by. Resolve conflicts quickly whenever possible, ask for *and grant* forgiveness before the offense has time to sit, take root, and grow into something that can become an unhealthy pattern in your marriage. If you and your mate are at an impasse, commit to each other that you will involve a third party as soon as possible to help resolve the conflict (either a counselor or mentor, for example). This will also help the meeker partner not to feel compelled to "give in" to an obstinate partner just to keep peace—then the root of the problem just gets swept under the rug only to reappear later. And always remember the rewards of making mistakes and having arguments: after things are resolved, you get to kiss and make up!

CHAPTER 6

KEEPING THE HONEYMOON ALIVE

Romance and

Intimacy

We're a military family who moves often—but nothing prepared us for the weather at Fort Drum in northern New York. While it's a beautiful part of the country and the summers are idyllic, the winters can be quite harsh. Gentle snowfalls can suddenly and without warning turn into violent storms.

On my way to pick up the five children from school one snowy day, I couldn't help but admire the slowly falling snow and the landscape of pure white it painted over the countryside barns and pastures. But after I picked up the children from the school and headed back toward home, the weather suddenly turned vicious, and the snowstorm became so fierce that traffic came to a standstill. We were trapped in what northerners call a "whiteout." With the temperature well below zero, I fought panic as a concerned chorus of children from the back of the car echoed out:

"Mom, how long are we going to be stuck here?"

"It's going to be awfully cold if we're here for hours."

"I can't see anything in front of us or to the side."

"What's going to happen to us?"

I glanced at the stranded vehicles beside and behind us and squinted (to no avail) to see more than three feet in front of us. I was totally disoriented and had no idea how far we were from home.

"Let's not panic! Kids, why don't we pray instead?" I answered, as we closed our eyes and momentarily shut out the ominous scene that was developing around us.

"God, please help us to see *just enough to get home*. Amen."

As *soon* as we opened our eyes, the children and I watched in amazement as the road in front of our vehicle cleared and the final stoplight before our house suddenly came into view like a beacon in the storm. We crept toward the light, eager to take advantage of the unusual break in the storm. Out of curiosity, I glanced into my rearview mirror, but no cars had followed us out of the storm—not one. It seemed as if the wintry veil had lifted just enough to get us home!

That adventurous day reminds me of a certain aspect of marriage—romance. After the perfect wedding and honeymoon, your relationship can seem so heavenly; everything is new and beautiful. Romantic love can be as gorgeous as an undisturbed mantle of gentle snow covering the fields on a winter's day. But storms are inevitable, and eventually something will happen to disturb the romantic bliss you've worked so carefully to maintain. And yet if you're prepared, you can weather the challenges that threaten the intimacy in your marriage.

The Language of Love

Part of being prepared for a fulfilling life of intimacy with your mate is understanding that sexual intimacy involves more than the physical. By nurturing your spouse emotionally, spiritually, and mentally, you can find more pleasure and fulfillment in all aspects of your intimate lives together.

A good place to start is simply with the language of love. In an *amazon.com* review of Gary Chapman's book *The Five Love Languages* (Northfield Publishers, 1992), the publisher comments:

Dr. Gary Chapman identifies these as the five languages of love: quality time, words of affirmation, gifts, acts of service, and physical touch. If you express love in a way your spouse doesn't understand, he or she won't realize you've expressed your love at all. The problem is that you're speaking two different languages. Perhaps your husband needs to hear encouraging words, but you feel cooking a nice dinner will cheer him up. When he still feels down, you're puzzled. Or maybe your wife craves time with you—time away from the kids and the television. The flowers you gave her just don't communicate that you care.

Here's my personal take on each of these love languages:

Quality Time Love to this person means taking time. It can be spent in conversation, on a walk, in a hobby activity, or just being together. When a person with this love language doesn't get to see their mate as much as they'd like, they begin to feel disconnected and unloved.

Words of Affirmation This means praise and not flattery. These people like to know when they've done something well and like to have their efforts verbally recognized. They also tend to be sensitive to criticism. They need to have twice as many positive words spoken to them as negative words.

Gifts A person who has this love language is not materialistic, they simply attach significance to tangible reminders of love. Consequently, gifts, cards, flowers, and books are all important to this person. That's why a forgotten birthday, Valentine's Day, or anniversary is especially difficult for someone with this love language.

Acts of Service This can be anything from doing the dishes to giving your mate a back massage. These folks spell love H-E-L-P, and in their language loving means *doing*.

Physical Touch If this is your love language and your mate is from a "touchy" family, then you two are off to a great start. But if you are not a particularly affectionate person by nature and your mate is, then it will be important for you to teach yourself to regularly rub a back, hold a hand, or stroke an arm. Sexual intimacy also tends to be more important to those who have this as their primary love language.

Bob and I read this book when it first came out ten years ago, and it helped our relationship tremendously. Bob's love language is words of affirmation and quality time but he thought my love language was acts of service. So when the kids were little, he'd bathe them, clean the kitchen, and vacuum. While I loved his help and appreciated it (and certainly wouldn't want him to stop), he thought he was speaking my love language. My love language is actually gifts, and I've always been wired this way. When I was younger, I thought I must be too materialistic because I was devastated when I got a cheap, last-minute gift. Later in life I realized that it communicated to me, "You are worth the price of a coffee cup bought at the airport, not a lasting, meaningful gift that requires forethought and a bit of a financial sacrifice."

> Let your spouse know what your love language is and seek to discover his.

So that's why a card and chocolate (gifts) on Valentine's Day is more important to me than Bob telling me he loves me (words of affirmation) or doing the dishes (acts of service). On the other hand, if I'm critical or short-tempered with Bob and just get quiet, it drives him crazy because his primary language is words of affirmation. Words affect him greatly and can be extremely helpful or extremely hurtful—so I've had to learn to be sensitive to his needs in this area.

If you want further study, get Dr. Chapman's excellent book and look at the different love languages. In the meantime, think about what most communicates love to you based on one (or more) of these five methods. Let your spouse know what your love language is and seek to discover his. Then your "conversations" in these five areas will be far more effective when you're speaking the right language.

The Components of Intimacy

True intimacy occurs in a marriage when the total person (mind, body, and emotions) is vulnerable before another and there is no shame present. It occurs when there are no barriers to loving each other in the way we need to be loved. We've already looked at several potential barriers that can hinder intimacy: a lack of understanding male/female differences, poor communication, or speaking the wrong love language. But when all the components of intimacy are present and functioning in a healthy manner, then our marriages can reach that highest level of communion.

Since we are complex beings, we need to consider all aspects of who we are that contribute to intimacy with our mate. If any of the basic components of intimacy are absent, complete intimacy cannot be achieved. There are four basic components of intimacy:

Component #1—The Body

When most people think of intimacy, they think of the physical aspect of touching, kissing, and, ultimately, sexual intercourse. But you may not realize that the body is actually designed to physically benefit from sexual intimacy. Shellie Arnold, a women's conference speaker and founder of *Return to Eden Ministries* (*www.returntoeden.net*), speaks in her seminar called "Healing for the Hurting Heart" about the physical benefits of sex. She says: "Our bodies are so complex with hormones and nerve endings and blood vessels. We are literally made, fashioned, and built to experience physical intimacy as a culmination of the other levels of intimacy. It all works together, and when it works well, boy, can it be fun!"

Shellie goes on to say, "Intimacy is cyclical. Physical intimacy facilitates intimacy in other areas, and vice versa. There are many benefits to having physical intimacy in a marriage." Some of the specific physical benefits are:

- Studies show that hormones released during sex relax us, reduce stress, and can improve the quality of sleep. (Michael F. Roizen, M.D., from *Real Age: Are You As Young As You Can Be?* Harper Collins Publishers, 1999).

- Statistics support the idea that the more sex you have the "younger" you are in your "body" years (Ibid.).
- For those with deep emotional scars from sexual abuse, issues of abandonment or other rejection, healthy sexual love can begin to touch those places that hurt and bring lasting healing.
- Studies show the hormones released during sex make a woman hypersensitive to touch and promote bonding with her mate. (Theresa Crenshaw, M.D., in *The Alchemy of Love and Lust: How Our Sex Hormones Influence Our Relationships*, Pocket Books, 1996).
- An orgasm increases blood flow to the extremities and can even help open your sinuses. In fact, Shellie says: "When I have a headache, I don't look for aspirin, I go find my husband!" (Linda Meeks, Philip Heit, and John Burt, *Education for Sexuality and HIV/AIDS*, Ohio: Meeks Heit Publishing Company, 1993).

> "When I have a headache, I don't look for aspirin, I go find my husband!"

So from the studies and from the experts, we see that a great way to begin to teach your mate how to love you is by showing him how to give you physical pleasure and by seeking how to do the same for him.

Component #2—The Emotions

This component directly relates to the number one need in women that we discussed in the previous chapter—affection. By giving his wife a casual kiss, holding her hand, and stroking her back throughout the day, a husband is feeding her emotional love tank and giving her the affection she needs. With a good emotional base, a woman is freer to respond to her husband in physical intimacy.

Likewise, if a husband is open with his emotions, sharing with his wife how he feels and inviting his wife into those inner parts of his mind and heart, he is becoming more emotionally intimate with his wife. When our husbands open up in this way, it goes against their natural grain that screams, "I'm a rock. I'm an island." So you must carefully respect his emotional vulnerability or he will once again shut you out of that part of himself.

Component #3—The Mind

It's been said that the most powerful sexual organ is the mind. The vast creativity that exists within our minds can bring us to a more intimate association with our spouse. The mind can be a help or a hindrance in physical intimacy. If we are so preoccupied with our schedule that we find our minds wandering over our "to-do" list—even in the middle of lovemaking— the mind can get in the way of intimacy. On the other hand, if we focus our minds on pleasuring each other, then it can heighten and increase sexual satisfaction.

A healthy mind also involves positive self-talk. Rather than focusing on physical flaws, think about the positive aspects of the body that you were created with. Don't tell yourself, "I'm not that gorgeous, I don't know what he sees in me." Say, "I'm so thankful that he loves to be with me and that makes me feel like a million bucks!"

Finally, it's important to watch what we shovel into our minds. If you tend to read fashion magazines and compare yourself to the women between the pages—then you'll *never* measure up. Likewise, a steady diet of soap operas or trashy love novels isn't going to add to your intimacy level with your husband, because *he* will never live up to that romantic ideal. Carefully monitor the movies, music, and magazines that you read and allow to be in your home—it will help you keep a healthy mindset.

Component #4—The Spirit

Do you and your husband connect on a spiritual level? Do you share the same values and convictions? The next chapter will discuss this topic in greater detail, but the spiritual connection is the "one flesh" part of marriage that completes the intimacy puzzle. When you connect on a spiritual level, it makes decision-making easier, it puts you on the same team, and it provides a strength that comes from without in order to bond the two of you together. God is that spiritual element that connects you to your husband, and the value of this is simply amazing.

Expectation and Experience

If you haven't done so already, it is important to look at your sexual past and how that contributes to your intimacy with your mate. This doesn't mean you have to disclose everything to your husband, unless it is traumatic, as in the case of sexual abuse. In that case, it is crucial (and without exception) that you speak with a trusted counselor, if you have not done so already. To find one of these counselors, use the applicable ideas we discussed on how to find a premarital counselor in chapter 1.

> Rather than focusing on physical flaws, think about the positive aspects of the body that you were created with.

You are bringing your sexual past, your attitudes about sex, and your sexual desire into this marriage relationship. Here are a few questions to ask yourself:

Experience   You may have experienced levels of intimacy that range from none to limited to extensive. If you have had no experience, then that's great—you really do have an advantage. Be sure you speak with your gynecologist about lubrication needs, soreness, bleeding, and other concerns. They are professionals, and they are there to answer your questions. If you have any other level of experience and carry guilt over some of your past actions, then you need to ask God and yourself for forgiveness and determine to move beyond your past. But keep in mind that other experiences will likely be difficult to forget. When they come to your mind, focus on your spouse and refuse to linger on past relationships. If you are having extreme difficulty in this area, you might consider seeing a family counselor of the same sex.

Expectation   It's important to look at what you expect from your married sexual relationship. Think about your drives and desires. Do you expect to have sex every day? Once a week? Do you expect the lovemaking session to last an hour or several hours? Should the lights always be low and the passions high? What do you have established in your mind as a successful sexual relationship? Keep in mind that you and your spouse will likely come to a mutual understanding over time of what is realistic and pleasing to you both.

You may have preconceived ideas about the purpose of sex. You may have grown up thinking sex is dirty, even in a marriage relationship (and even if you think sex is great, the following book can help you make it better). I encourage you to read *Pure Passion* (Intervarsity Press, 1994) by Bill and Pam Farrel and Jim and Sally Conway. They state the basic premise of the book in the introduction: "The sexual revolution kicked the sides out of the morality box. But as inhibitions escaped, so did the ability to maintain an ongoing, pleasurable, intimate relationship. There were no handles to help us hold onto love.

Focus on your spouse and refuse to linger on past relationships.

It is our hope that this book can be a 'heart hold' so you can experience pure pleasure and make your marriage a great affair."

A Five-Star Lover

There's a great little book called *Marriage Moments: Heart-to-Heart Times to Deepen Your Love* (Servant Publications, 1998) by David and Claudia Arp. Bob and I read this devotional and were challenged to become even better lovers for each other after we read it. Here are what the Arps describe as the top characteristics of a great lover.

Exclusivity Your spouse is a gift from God for you to enjoy exclusive of any other kind of relationship. We need to affirm absolute loyalty to our mate.

Other-Centered A great lover seeks to meet the needs of the other first, and in doing so finds that there is great sexual satisfaction in fulfilling our mate. Your goal should be to please each other. It also means that we are honest but never unkind.

Multidimensional This encompasses all the dimensions of intimacy that we've discussed so far. In an effort to stress the physical aspect of the sexual relationship, it might be easy to overlook the fact that a healthy love life requires more than this one dimension of interaction. It also requires emotional and spiritual intimacy. But it can also mean that we have fun with our mates, which energizes the relationship.

Homework: Bonds of Intimacy

There's nothing like practice to make perfect, so here's a quick list to review and see where you can begin to apply some of the principles of intimacy with your spouse—starting tonight. The following is taken from Ed Wheat's bestselling book *Love Life for Every Married Couple* (Zondervan, 1997).

- physical touching of an affectionate, nonsexual nature
- shared feelings
- closeness without inhibitions
- absence of psychological defenses
- open communication and honesty
- intellectual agreement on major issues
- spiritual harmony
- sensitive appreciation of the mate's physical and emotional responses
- imparted secrets
- genuine understanding
- mutual confidence
- a sense of warmth, safety, and realization when together
- sensuous nearness
- sexual pleasures lovingly shared
- signs of love freely given and received
- mutual responsibility and caring
- abiding trust

But there's one more thing you need to keep in mind about marital intimacy. This final aspect has to do with the natural stages a marriage goes through. Marriage therapist Michele Weiner-Davis wrote about this in a *Parade* magazine article (March 17, 2002). She said: "I can tell you that what happens in marriage is surprisingly predictable, and couples familiar with the emotional terrain ahead are better able to handle the bumpy roads."

She goes on to describe the basic stages, which vary in length. Stage one is where you likely are right now: head over heels in love. It's easy to overlook your differences and at no other time will your physical passion be as intense as it is now. While it's great to enjoy the magic, it's also important to realize that the euphoria won't last forever. Weiner-Davis says, "When it [physical passion] starts to fade, remember: Your marriage isn't failing. Infatuation is not the glue that holds marriages together."

But hang in there as you head into stage two, where reality sets in, differences become glaring, and the passion begins to settle down into a more predictable pattern. Just keep the lines of communication open, practice good conflict resolution skills, and continue to make a robust sex life one of your top priorities. And life will be good.

CHAPTER 7

CRAFTING A SPIRITUAL FOUNDATION

How to Develop a Spiritual

Bond That Won't Be Broken

We attended the wedding of a young man who worked for Bob, and it was an experience I'll never forget. The young man's fiancée made him leave the Air Force Academy in order to marry her (you can't be married and attend the Academy). So he left his dream of becoming an officer for his new "chief of staff." But it was only an omen of things to come.

We'll call our friend Carlos. I'll never forget how uncomfortable I was when Carlos told his friends who were at the wedding, "Just don't say anything to Maria. Don't look at her and don't talk to her—or she might get mad!"

We couldn't believe it! Was this girl going to be high maintenance, or what?

By the time we got seated in the Catholic church, the wedding processional was just about

to begin. In typical Hispanic style, there were twelve bridal attendants and the same number of groomsmen. It was a huge wedding with elaborate flowers, decorations, and a spectacular reception planned. There was only one thing missing: a *happy* bride.

Oh, there was a bride, all right, but she was far from happy. Apparently someone looked at her or talked to her.

In Hispanic tradition, the bride and groom walk down the aisle together during the processional. So Carlos entered the church with Maria on his arm. They walked in short steps, then paused together;

step ... together ... all the way up the aisle.

You could see her flushed face even under the veil. It was clear she was very angry. She grabbed Carlos' arm and dug her nails into his sleeve. She had a word to speak at every step.

Step ... together

"Porque tu amiga me mira de esa forma?"

Step ... together

"Estoy muy irritada, porque debias de haber preguntado antes de invitarla."

Step ... together

"Te arrepentiras de haberlo hecho?"

Yep. For those of you who aren't fluent in Spanish, the translation was: The groom was in deep *kimche* and he knew it. All his friends who were rooting for him to become the "Runaway Groom" had to hightail it out of the church.

Can you believe starting out your marriage in front of God, family, and friends on that kind of footing? It was amazing. The bride and groom had not yet started their married life together, and they were already out of step!

Time bore witness to the fact that Maria would try to control every aspect of her marriage and family—from how the money was spent to what their religious affiliation and participation would involve. Her husband was not the head of his home in regard to critical issues of finances and faith. His wife became the spiritual head of the home, and he eventually lost interest in matters of faith.

It is so important to have a firm spiritual foundation from which you can craft a life together in order to weather the inevitable storms of life. Here are a few areas that will help you get started on that foundation.

Why Church? I Can Find God in a Tree!

Yeah, but a tree can't talk to you, tell you how to work through conflict, or pray for you when you need prayer. When it comes to attending church, some people believe that they don't need to go to a building to commune with God—and we don't. But all of us are social beings with a spiritual makeup, which is the key to who we are as individuals. We need the fellowship, encouragement, and wisdom that are found within the walls of a church.

Fellowship   A young boy who was afraid of the dark told his mom that it wasn't enough that God was with him in the scary room; he said, "I want God with skin on!" That's what's at the heart of basic fellowship.

Encouragement   There are two sides to this coin: the first is the "feel good" kind of encouragement that comes from the inspiration of courage and hope that we observe in the lives of other people. That kind of support is the first side of the coin—the one that most of us think of when we hear the word. However, the other side of encouragement has to do with a loving resolve from others who will tell us the truth in love. If we're slamming our husbands in public, and thus damaging their self-esteem right along with the marriage—then we need someone who will encourage us to get a grip. We all need friends who will give us the hard word of Proverbs: "Faithful are the wounds of a friend." We are likely to find this—with a diligent search—in a church environment from people who have the same values and goals.

> We need the fellowship, encouragement, and wisdom that are found within the walls of a church.

Wisdom   There's another Proverb that says, "There is wisdom in many counselors." This *doesn't* mean we go running from one person to another—gathering their ideas as if we're taking a poll on how we should solve our problems. We are talking about developing a relationship with another couple or same-sex person whom you respect and admire. We are likely to find these people, who can serve as role models as well as wise counselors, in a church. We get to choose whom to ask to pray for us and from whom to ask advice. We get to choose which advice we'll take. And because we don't have all the answers, it's important that we ask. In a healthy, thriving church, wisdom is readily available all the way from the pulpit to the pews.

Choosy Couples Choose a Church

In the '80s there was a popular television commercial that said, "Choosey moms choose Jif." The implication was that if you care about your kids' peanut butter, you'll choose the best. Well, I imagine that choosing a church is a slightly higher priority than choosing a sandwich filler. Couples will sometimes get frustrated searching for a church that has the kind of theology, ministry philosophy, program, and style that they are looking for. Then they do the worst thing they can do—they give up looking for a church and get into a habit of forgoing this incredible source of fellowship, encouragement, and wisdom.

A good start in helping you sort out the issues and choose the right church for you is to ask the right questions. Check the Yellow Pages for church descriptions and start calling—most of the basic questions can be answered over the phone and will save you the time of visiting churches that don't meet your needs. Or, do an Internet search on churches in your area; much of this information is posted online. You can also use the Internet to begin researching churches *before* you move to a new area to narrow down a list of churches you'll want to visit when you arrive. Either way, here are the topics you'll want to cover.

What is the basic worship style? The three basic styles of worship are liturgical, traditional, and contemporary. The style of worship will largely reflect the values, emphasis, and target audience (who they want to minister to). There are not any right or wrong styles, but you'll need to find one that both of you are comfortable with.

What are their doctrinal beliefs? This is not a question of preference or style, it's a fundamental question of how they interpret the Bible, what they believe it says, how it should govern our lives, and how we are to live accordingly.

What is their mission statement? Most churches have a mission statement posted on their Web site or available upon request. This brochure or printout will answer many of the questions raised in this section and will give you very clear guidance as to what a particular church believes and what their goals are.

What is their reputation? We've moved so many times since we've been married that we're professional church shoppers. Once we heard that a pastor from a certain church was a very loud preacher, and Bob immediately decided that his sensitive hearing couldn't handle that. We floundered for a year, and then ended up in this church we wouldn't visit previously because of its so-called reputation. If you hear talk about a church—good or bad—consider the source, ask follow-up questions, and call or visit personally in order to confirm or deny that information.

What programs and opportunities for service exist? If you are looking for a contemporary church service that has a Saturday evening option so you can have Sundays free—call and find out their program schedule, or ask them to mail you a church bulletin. Do they have a couple's fellowship class? Do they offer marital counseling? Do they have a viable youth program that you could help with?

What's the basic size of the church? If it is huge, but offers small cell groups, then you will need to know this in order to make an informed decision. Some people like bigger churches and find a place of belonging in their Sunday school class or home fellowship—while others feel big churches are impersonal. This is a phone question. We had some friends who were looking for a mid-size church and began selecting churches out of the phone book based on their descriptions but didn't call any of them first. Consequently, they spent several Sunday mornings driving up to a "church" that turned out to be a mobile home or worse, and driving right back out of the parking lot. Do your homework, and you won't waste your Sundays.

What is the church government? There are three basic forms of church government: congregational rule, pastoral rule, or elder rule. Some feel more comfortable with a pastor who can make his own decisions and not cater to a board. However, others feel the accountability of a board makes for higher quality decisions.

What is the pastor's leadership style? Some are preachers, some have lots of guests in the pulpit, and others are more like teachers. Some are highly involved and others prefer to delegate. All these factors determine the church's leadership style.

What are the membership requirements? Some churches have no formal membership at all while others require prospective members to attend an eight-week class. Some churches have stringent requirements of its members and actually require members to tithe in order to join, or abstain from all alcohol, or send their kids to the church school, etc. Find out what the requirements for membership are long before you decide to join.

News Alert:
THERE IS NO
PERFECT CHURCH.

What does the church "feel" like? "Feelings, whoa, whoa, whoa, feelings." While life is best lived when not based on feelings, the feel of a church has everything to do with your choice. Is it quiet and reverential, or loud and filled with activity? Do you feel that visitors are welcome, or do you think you could be there fifteen years and never quite be "one of them." (Don't laugh; we attended a church where the people were nice until we officially became members; then we were treated like transients. We transitioned right on out of there.)

Can I live with them? News Alert: THERE IS NO PERFECT CHURCH. Once you realize this, you'll stop majoring on the minors and look at the big world-picture of a particular church. The main question is: Can I live with the things that I don't like about this church? Maybe they sing the first, second, and fourth stanzas instead of all of the verses in a song. Maybe the pastor wears a robe, and your childhood pastor never wore a robe. Are these issues you can overcome, or not?

Interdependent Versus Independent Spirituality

Basically church attendance is the primary form of interdependent spirituality, but what about independent spirituality? It's important that we take responsibility for our own relationship with God. We aren't responsible for our mate's spiritual status—and they aren't responsible for ours; neither is your mama or daddy responsible. We may have had negative experiences in religious contexts in the past; however, we cannot let those past grievances define our spiritual lives today. We don't give up on God, because He hasn't given up on us. And while you cannot control your mate's spirituality, you can do something about your own by developing some personal spiritual disciplines that will help you in this life.

Independent Disciplines

An excellent classic book on the disciplines is *A Celebration of Discipline* by Richard Foster (HarperCollins, 1978, 1998, 1). He calls these the "inward disciplines," which begin with the premise "Superficiality is the curse of our age. The doctrine of instant satisfaction is a primary spiritual problem. The desperate need today is not for a greater number of intelligent people, or gifted people, but for deep people."

> **While you cannot control your mate's spirituality, you can do something about your own.**

The inward disciplines are a fantastic tool for us in our independent desire to work on our individual spiritual lives. They are: meditation, prayer, fasting, and study. Let's look at them a bit closer.

Meditation Psychiatrist Carl Jung once said, "Hurry is not *of* the Devil; it *is* the Devil." We need to slow down long enough to contemplate the things of God and to hear and obey His voice. True meditation is not so much detaching one's self from life by emptying ourselves as it is that we become *attached* to God and learn to hear Him speak into our lives. It is a communion between man and God as we read His words in the Bible, think deeply about them, and then listen.

Prayer Foster says, "Prayer catapults us onto the frontier of the spiritual life.... Meditation introduces us to the inner life, fasting is an accompanying means, study transforms our minds, but it is the discipline of prayer that brings us into the deepest and highest work of the human spirit ... to pray is to change." It's not so much that prayer changes our spouse as it is that prayer changes us. It causes us to become more *God*-focused and less *self*-focused. We explore new areas of faith by talking to God openly and honestly and then listening to His reply.

Fasting This is a lost art that is regaining popularity. Spiritual fasting is never for the purpose of losing weight, but it is for spiritual purposes. Foster explains it: "We cover up what is inside us with food and other good things, but in fasting these things surface. If pride controls us, it will be revealed almost immediately . . . anger, bitterness, jealousy, strife, fear—if they are within us, they will surface during fasting." So fasting is, by design, a discipline that helps us look at the areas that need to be changed and to strengthen those positive areas that are already established. For more information on this topic, read Foster's book.

Study We've already recommended some good books that will take you into a deeper spiritual life, but the Bible is the bestseller of all time, and it's the best place to start. Foster goes on to say that the four steps of effective study are: repetition (which focuses the mind in a specific direction), concentration, comprehension, and reflection. The wisdom literature of the Psalms and Proverbs is a great text to study. Personally, I read every thirtieth chapter of Psalms daily and the corresponding Proverb. So on the fifth of the month, I study Psalms 5, 35, 65, 95, and 125, and Proverbs 5. You can also study books such as *Experiencing God Together* by Dr. David Stoop (Tyndale, 1996) or *Into the Depths of God* by Calvin Miller (Bethany House Publishers, 2001).

Personal Renewal

It's hard to isolate a part of who we are: for example, our spiritual lives, and call it exclusively "independent," because it is highly interdependent upon other areas of our lives. While fellowship is interdependent and the spiritual disciplines are independent, the need for personal renewal is one that affects our entire self: physically, emotionally, mentally, and spiritually. So if we only focus on our spiritual lives to the exclusion of the other areas, we will miss the point of personal renewal. Let's take a quick look at each of these elements that are necessary for vibrant personal health.

Physical

I once heard a very well-known, highly conservative evangelist in the '80s preach against the use of birth control. When he was asked about the effects on the health of a woman who has eight children in ten years, and the subsequent weight gain, he responded, "Well, she can just have all her children, then when she's through, she can go on a crash diet and lose eighty pounds!" He was serious.

> **If our body is the "temple of the Holy Spirit," we ought to take good care of it.**

Our physical well-being is, in some ways, a reflection of our spiritual status. If our body is the "temple of the Holy Spirit," we ought to take good care of it. By exercising, eating healthy foods, and managing stress, we are better able to serve others and meet their spiritual needs, as well. I know that, personally, I have to work out in order to keep my energy level up. I've always done this—even when the five kids were seven and under. I'd put two children in the double stroller, one would be on his bicycle, the toddler was strapped on my backpack, and the newborn was in a swaddle across my chest. I carried forty pounds of children and pushed another eighty pounds of kids, but by golly, I got my workout!

Emotional

This part of our makeup also blends into the social aspects of who we are. I have found that healthy friendships with my girl friends are one of the greatest things I can do for my emotional health. While Bob is my best friend, he's not a woman (which I appreciate greatly at times). I need the outlet of these friendships in which I can vent, laugh, and be encouraged. I also stop to *listen* to my girl friends when they need to talk. Lasting friendships are about giving and taking, and we need both. Speaking of giving . . .

When I'm going through a personal crisis or feeling depressed, one of the best things I can do is to reach out to others. Sometimes we help a friend through their problems and forget our own. Another thing I do is to volunteer at the homeless shelter, and I have done all kinds of different acts of service throughout the years. It keeps me emotionally healthy to forget about my problems for a while and reach out to help someone else with hers.

Mental

When I went to Colorado Christian University (CCU) to get a degree in the management of human resources, little did I know I would one day be managing *so many* little human resources!

Once you're done with school, and especially if you ever stay home with your children one day, it's very easy to fall into a rut and neglect this part of your psyche. But remaining healthy mentally is vitally important to who you are, and in the long run—to your marriage. In my CCU class, there was a woman named Madeline who was seventy years old! She'd never finished her degree and wanted to do it, so she did. I think of Madeline every now and then, and she is an inspiration to me still.

Reading, using your imagination to dream dreams and problem solve, planning for the future, engaging in creative writing, developing new talents, and learning new skills are all part of developing your mind. Sometimes you never know what you are intellectually capable of until you try. Join the local Toastmasters and learn to give a speech. Go to a writer's conference and learn how to write fiction. Take a pottery, painting, or French class. Join a local book critique class—you get the idea.

To Pray (Together) or Not to Pray?

I've left this topic for last, although you may be wondering why it wasn't first, because shared prayer seems like it would be a priority in the spiritual foundation of a marriage. It is. But it's hard. I'll never forget when I learned how "together prayer" impacted Bob. We'd been married *ten years* and were sitting in a couples' Sunday school class. The discussion was about guys praying with their wives, and Bob said, "I've always been intimidated by praying out loud with Ellie, but I've finally forced myself to do it. She knows more about the Bible than I do, and I've always been kind of reserved about praying together." Wow!

I've since learned that Bob isn't alone; a lot of guys don't feel comfortable praying out loud with their wives. But, hopefully, just like the World's Greatest Fighter Pilot, they will venture into this strange new world and at least give it a try. Eventually it can become easier for them because it is important to have the common place of release and renewal that prayer offers.

Dr. David Stoop, a clinical psychologist and seminary professor, said in *Experiencing God Together* (Tyndale, 1996) something that also surprised me about husbands and wives that study the Bible together. In his radio program one day, he got a call from a woman who was frustrated by the way she and her husband studied together. She said it wasn't improving their spiritual intimacy at all. When questioned, she revealed that her husband was always the teacher and she was always the student, and then exploded with: "Not only is he always the teacher, he isn't a very good teacher. He's always got to be right. My opinions mean nothing to him. It usually ends up with his telling me what I'm supposed to be learning, and I sit there silently angry."

But that isn't the part of the story I found to be remarkable. It was Dr. Stoop's reply: "I know very few couples who can handle doing a formal Bible study together. The teacher/ student arrangement certainly isn't conducive to a growing sense of partnership! And partnership is what the spiritual disciplines within marriage are meant to build." He went on to say that both partners should be the students, and the Holy Spirit should be the teacher in any effective study.

There's a natural temptation within each of us to compare our situation with others. You may see a man who seems to be a spiritual giant and wish your hubby was the same. Comparisons rarely lead to renewal. So why not let yourself and your guy off the hook when it comes to joint prayer and study? Don't concentrate on what your husband *isn't doing* in the spiritual arena—concentrate on your own spiritual life and highlight and praise the areas (even if they're limited) where your husband is doing well.

If you want to pursue this subject with further reading, take a look at Stormie Omartian's bestselling books *The Power of a Praying Wife* (Harvest House, 1997) and *The Power of a Praying Husband* (Harvest House, 2001).

Every family needs a leader in the area of spirituality, and this is the basic premise of a book by James Walker called *Husbands Who Won't Lead and Wives Who Won't Follow* (Bethany House Publishers, 2000, 10). Walker says,

> Some husbands become passive or uncertain about their leadership role. Consequently, wives may unavoidably take on responsibilities they'd rather not bear. For others, the time pressure and distractions of modern life have eroded the energy, attention, and patience so vital to sustaining a healthy marriage.

This brings us back to our story from the beginning of this chapter where the wife ruled supreme and would not consider her husband's leadership in the home. This is a critical balance where the wife appreciates her husband's input but she is never made to feel subservient in the relationship. One person has to be responsible for final decisions, but it should be a joint effort in the process. This is especially true when it comes to spiritual matters. It is sometimes easier for husbands and wives to agree on how many children to have than where they will go to church and how often. But our spiritual lives need to become a priority in order to combat the daily issues of life.

Don't let time pressures or modern-day distractions erode your spiritual lives. Your spiritual bonds are the most intimate aspects of your relationship. Building a firm spiritual foundation requires a lot of effort and energy, but your marriage is worth it.

Queen of Everything

Building Your Home

CHAPTER 8

Born Spender Marries Born Saver

How to Take Control of Your Finances

I get more mileage out of a quarter than a Hyundai gets out of a gas can. You see, I'm a born saver. I started saving money so early in life that by the time I was twelve years old I'd saved enough to fund a trip to Spain to visit my cousins. I took three rolls of film with me and only snapped six pictures, thereby "saving" two and one-half rolls! Okay, I guess I used to be a little compulsive about saving. I know how to save money so well that I built a career around teaching others how to do things like feed a family of seven for only $250 a month, pay down debt, and establish a workable family budget.

On the other hand, my husband, Bob, is a born spender. When he was a kid, his paper route money never saw the inside of his pocket. This pattern continued into his adult years, and when he became a fighter pilot in the Air Force, he could still spend money faster than his Stealth F–117 could go from zero to 500 mph. For you Air Force novices, that's pretty fast!

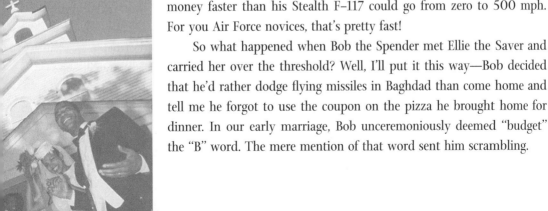

So what happened when Bob the Spender met Ellie the Saver and carried her over the threshold? Well, I'll put it this way—Bob decided that he'd rather dodge flying missiles in Baghdad than come home and tell me he forgot to use the coupon on the pizza he brought home for dinner. In our early marriage, Bob unceremoniously deemed "budget" the "B" word. The mere mention of that word sent him scrambling.

Now, don't get me wrong! Bob and I have a lot in common—we both enjoy gourmet coffee and dark chocolate and we like scoping out our new digs after yet another military move. When we fly, both of us also like to rate the pilot's landing on a scale of one to ten. Oddly, we always rate the landings the same (most pilots average a seven in our book). As a matter of fact, we agreed on just about everything when we got married—except money. And yet we wanted to manage our finances together as well as we rated a pilot's landing.

Bob and I are not the only couple with contrasting viewpoints when it comes to money. Finances are mentioned as the number one topic couples argue about in marriage, and money problems are cited for most divorces according to popular surveys. Money matters can be a real problem in family life, even if two "savers" are married to each other, because they still have to decide on their financial goals and priorities. We found that an effective tool to work out our financial differences was that dreaded "B" word: budget.

Bob and I knew that if we didn't get a firm grip on our opposing approaches to money management, we'd have to face some ugly consequences one day—like juggling bills and nasty calls from bill collectors. And yet an overemphasis on "saving" would only cause stress on the family. As the saver, I had to adjust my expectations for Bob: was it reasonable for me to demand we go to McDonald's *only on Tuesdays,* when they offer 99¢ Happy Meals—and no other time? Of course not! Was it all right for Bob to go out and buy a $500 tool chest and $1,000 worth of tools to go in it on the outside chance he might need them one day—and put it all on a credit card because we didn't have cash for the purchase? Of course not! Yes, we both needed to get a grip.

It wasn't easy for the spender in our relationship to get into the budget habit. We had some harrowing takeoffs and hit pockets of turbulence while attempting to "fly straight" financially. Initially we went off and on our budget, struggling one month, doing it right the next. I once blew up at Bob for buying a used VCR for $25 that actually worked quite well. I had wanted him to check the Consumer Guide before making purchases like that! No, it certainly wasn't clear skies at first, but eventually, with prayer and perseverance, both of us found balance—and peace once again reigned in our home.

If financial health is one of the goals for your marriage, the best thing you can do is to establish a workable household budget. The following tips can help you establish a working outline for your finances. With a little creativity, prayer, and some hard work, you can aim high and fly with the best.

Top-Ten Tips for a Workable Household Budget

Assess Current Spending/Saving

At the end of this chapter, I've provided a budget form. You may make photocopies of it and fill in the blanks for your "current spending" levels. Be sure to record all debt accumulation, including credit cards and "hidden bills." Read the "Hidden Bills" and "Still More Hidden Bills" sections that follow.

> If financial health is one of the goals for your marriage, the best thing you can do is to establish a workable household budget.

As a matter of fact, it's a good idea to read the rest of this chapter to unearth all those hidden debts before you complete the chart.

Since the goal is to live *below* your means, you will need to also allocate money for specific savings areas, and you'll see those on the chart as well. If you're already saving, then you're ahead in the budget game.

Assess Net Income

This is the household income *after* state and federal income taxes and Social Security. Income includes salary, rents, notes, interest, dividends, income tax refunds, and other forms of income. Enter the total on the "Net Income" line on the budget form included in this section.

Where Are You?

Now take your net income and subtract your current spending to establish your overall family spending. Are you spending more (through credit) than you make each month? Are you spending everything you make (with nothing going into savings)? Are there unexplained gaps in your current spending levels? Did you know you were hitting the ATM machine that many times each month? Are you saving as much as you'd like to?

You have to start at the beginning, and the first three tips help you know where you are so you can have a better idea of where you're going.

Projected Budget

Look on the budget chart and fill in the "projected budget" column according to the percentage given. These figures are based on an average American's household income of between $20,000 and $38,000 a year. The percentages are guidelines and will vary according to family size, geographic location, and income.

This column gives a good idea of where to go with your budget. Take the difference between columns one and two to determine if your current spending levels are over or under the projected budget. Compare your current spending column with the projected budget column to determine areas that need the most attention in your budget. Write the difference (either in the black or in the red) in column three.

Actual Budget

Using the projected budget as a guideline, tailor an actual budget for your family. For example, you might drive a company car, so your automobile expenses would be lower than average. You could take this overage and apply it to the servicing of consumer debt. Or you may need to take measures to cut your food budget or shop around on insurance to arrive at a workable overall budget for your family.

Your expenses may vary according to your geographical location. People living in the North may have higher utility bills due to the harsh winters. People in the South may have a greater electricity bill due to air conditioning in the summer. Our family has higher education costs because of the number of children in our family.

A "couple meeting" is the best place to establish this budget and make the commitment to stick to it. This meeting can be a fun time for you and your spouse. Make some popcorn, or have dessert and coffee, and approach it from a positive direction.

Hidden Bills

These are expenses that should be figured into the monthly budget in order to give an accurate assessment of where you're at in annual expenses. These include bills that may not come due on a monthly basis. Nevertheless, the budget should provide for the payment of those items. These debts also include insurance premiums, property and other taxes, retail credit, money owed to family and friends, doctor and dentist bills, magazine subscriptions, etc. There are blank spaces on the budget worksheet to fill in these expenses.

Still More Hidden Bills

Each category in the worksheet has hidden expenses you may not have considered. This is a complete, itemized list of costs that should be included in each of these categories.

Tithe/Charitable Donations Church, civic, and community donations.

Savings Savings accounts, savings for hidden debts, and unexpected emergencies.

Clothing/Dry Cleaning New clothing and shoes, thrift store bargains, garage sale finds, dry cleaning, alterations, repairs, patterns and other sewing supplies.

Education/Miscellaneous Tuition, books, music or other lessons, school supplies, newspaper, and miscellaneous expenses. The miscellaneous portion includes all unbudgeted items and any debt payments.

Food Groceries, and meals eaten outside the home.

Housing Includes mortgage or rent, property taxes, utilities (including phone, gas, water, and electricity), cleaning supplies, labor costs/maid, lawn care, pool care, tools and repair, stationery, postage, household repairs, furniture and bedding, appliances, and garden equipment.

Insurance   The percentage provided assumes some employee insurance benefits. It also includes life, homeowner's, and health insurance.

Medical/Dental   Doctor, dentist, eyeglasses, medicines, and vitamins.

Recreation/Vacation/Gifts and Christmas   Cameras and film, entertainment, movies, hobbies, pets, television, sporting goods, toys, all gifts, Christmas decorations and gifts, and vacations.

Transportation   Airline fares, bus and taxi fares, car payments and insurance, car repairs and licenses, gasoline and oil.

Budget Busters

There are a few problem areas that can throw a budget off course in a matter of seconds—sending it reeling toward disaster. The use of credit, or debt, is the number one budget buster. If overspending is an issue, you may want to look at making your policy one of "cash only." Some couples set up an envelope system for cash. Every two weeks they place the budgeted amount of cash in envelopes marked "food," "entertainment," "gas," etc. When the money runs out—you're done, until the end of the two-week period. A regular peek at the amount of cash left in each envelope is a vivid reminder of your budget commitments.

If you don't have the cash for that gorgeous new outfit on sale at your favorite store, then don't buy it. If you really can't afford to go out to eat four times a month, then go only twice. If it's not in your budget to fly out to your mother's for vacation, then drive, or let Mom come to you. "Cash only" is an important principle in sticking to an effective budget.

More Budget Busters

Impulse buying, as we've discussed earlier, is a temptation faced by almost everyone. Whether it's a candy bar or a Corvette—we've all given in to the craving at one time or another. There are ways to short-circuit this tendency within our natures, and one of the best ways is the "thirty-day plan." If it's not in your budget, then wait thirty days, thereby delaying the purchase. During that month, find two other items that are similar and compare prices. If it's still available at a good price and it fits the next month's budget, buy it. What I think you'll find is that you're buying less stuff, because this delay gives you the opportunity to get beyond the impulse.

Make it your policy to never use credit cards for impulse purchases. As a matter of fact, it's best to leave your credit cards at home. Don't even carry them to the mall or to the store. If you have a problem in this area, then you may need to take this impulse-buying detonation process one step further—don't shop. Hightail it on out of the mall and the stores; that's where the majority of impulse purchases occur in the first place. If an alcoholic should avoid bars, then a shopaholic should avoid malls.

> **The use of debt, or credit, is the number one budget buster.**

Still More Budget Busters

The final area that busts a budget is gifts. Think about the gifts you buy for relatives, baby showers, weddings, birthdays, Valentine's Day, Mother's Day, Father's Day, kids' birthdays, and anniversaries. In the military we also have welcome gifts, farewells, pin-on's, hospitality, and the list goes on for both of us. And this doesn't even cover the biggie—Christmas. But we'll have more on that in chapter 12.

The first thing we should do is evaluate the "why" of gift giving. Do we really have to give a material gift in every circumstance? Wouldn't a card work just as well in some cases? What about baked goods? Occasionally the giving of a gift puts the other person under a sense of obligation. Are you putting more emphasis on the gift than the giver? It is, after all, the thought that counts.

One of the ways to save on gifts is to make or bake some of them. I value handmade or homemade gifts, because I know the time and effort that goes into them. I only handcraft a few special gifts for very special people—because my time is also a gift. All my welcome and hospitality gifts are baked goods. I've yet to have someone turn up their nose at a hot loaf of honey wheat bread given as a hospitality present.

I keep a calendar of special events and dates. If I'm making a cross-stitch or other craft for that special day, marking the start time/complete time of the project on my calendar helps. Gathering the gifts that need to be mailed in advance of the special day helps avoid a priority postage charge.

Whether you're a born spender or a born saver, it's important to agree on a workable household budget. It's much easier to stick to a plan that you've both agreed on, and one that has some flex here and there. But remember! When you buy pizza, use a coupon!

BUDGET PAYMENT PER MONTH							
ACCOUNT NAME	**CURRENT SPENDING**		**PROJECTED BUDGET**		**DIFFERENCE**		**ACTUAL BUDGET**
Tithes/contributions (10%)							
Savings (10%)							
Clothing/Dry Cleaning (5%)							
Education/Misc. (5%)							
Food (10%)							
Housing/Utilities/Taxes (30%)							
Insurance (5%)							
Medical/Dental (4%)							
Recreation/Vacation							
Gifts/Christmas (6%)							
Transportation (15%)							
Total							
Net Income							
Difference							

CHAPTER 9

THE SAVINGS QUEEN REIGNS!

How to Shop, Save, and Share Your Way to Marital Bliss

When *Shop, Save, and Share* was released, I was dubbed "The Savings Queen," and I made my national television debut on James and Betty Robison's *Life Today* show. The ministry produced a video based upon my book to raise money for needy children in underdeveloped countries. We did a lot of on-location filming, and naturally one of those locations was the grocery store.

James Robison's daughter, Rhonda, helped with the taping as I took her around the grocery store, giving her instructions on how to shop wisely and save lots of money. She has four children, and found my approach to grocery shopping to be effective in cutting costs for her family. She is a self-admitted "grocery nomad," so we filmed her wandering around the store

with a blank look on her face, muttering, "Now, where is the peanut butter?"

We also talked the store manager into delivering a line at the checkout counter. It was also his national television debut. As the cameras rolled, Rhonda asked me, "What do the checkers say when you go through their line and they see how much you've saved?"

I answered, "Well, Rhonda, some of them scream and run for the break room, but most of them say..."

The camera panned to the store manager, who was still standing by the register, and he said, (drum roll, please) "Wow! *I* need to use coupons!"

By this time, there were a lot of customers at the checkouts watching the commotion and wondering what in the world was going on with the woman wearing a crown and being followed by cameramen and a production crew.

There was one final shot of us pushing the cart out of the store. As I walked by the crowds of people waiting at the checkouts, I gave my best Elizabethan "royal wave." I felt like I was in the scene from *The Sound of Music* where the patrons of a ball wave good-bye to the Von Trapp children.

The camera panned the customers and checkers, most of whom gave us the royal wave in return, while some just stared. Can you imagine what you'd do if you'd just run to the store to grab some milk and encountered a "savings queen" with her entourage? It would make for interesting dinner conversation.

There is no more comprehensive book on grocery shopping than my book *Shop, Save, and Share*. It is a master's course on how to find, swap, organize, use, combine, and double every type of coupon (store, manufacturer's, instant, competitor's, etc.) for maximum savings. It also covers in detail how to save money in many other areas, such as cars, clothing, furniture, and appliances. If you want to take this chapter to the next level in saving money, that book is required reading. If you start now to make savings a habit, it will serve you well for years to come. Here are some of my favorite tips:

How to Save on Groceries

Menus

One of the most commonly asked questions is "Do you plan menus for the week?"
My answer is "I plan my menus according to what I have in my pantry."
Since the majority of things I buy are purchased on sale and with a coupon, I know I've

paid the lowest price possible for those products in my pantry.

In the menu approach, you decide what you will eat for the week and then are committed to buying those items whether you have a coupon or not and whether they are on sale or not.

Using the *Shop, Save, and Share* method, I may have to supplement a *few* items like cottage cheese or fresh tomatoes. But I usually have the vast majority of the items I will need already in stock. Therefore, I will save more money than with the menu-plan approach to grocery shopping.

If you start now to make savings a habit, it will serve you well for years to come.

Milk, Meat, and Produce

Another commonly asked question is "What do you do about meat, milk, and produce? I rarely find coupons for those items."

For meat, buy when it's on sale and stock up. Even if you don't have a terribly large freezer, you can still prioritize and maximize your freezer space by packing items in plastic freezer bags or freezer containers. Then you'll have room for chicken breasts when they go on sale for 79¢ a pound.

I usually buy milk wherever it is on sale. Since most people buy this staple every week, it is usually on sale somewhere in your town. If you don't want to make a trip to the store just for the sale-priced milk, check to see if the store you are going to has a policy for "honoring competitor's ads."

Many Wal-Mart Superstores will honor all competitors' ads. All you have to do is take in the competitor's ad with the sale price on any of the items you want. Check with the store manager, but they usually substitute other store brands with their own brand. For example, I had an ad for twelve packs of IGA brand soda in the sale circular I brought to Wal-Mart. They substituted their Sam's brand for that soda, and I got it for the sale price.

Most stores that offer this additional service do have some restrictions. They will usually not honor advertised store coupons, percentage discounts, or buy one/get one free specials. But it is still worth your time (and money) to ask the right questions at your local store.

E-mail Clubs

These are designed to help you find the best values *locally* within your own community. I was a member of a highly successful e-mail club in northern New York that passes on not only the local news but also news on freebies that are found on the Internet. I've heard about free coffee, postage, baby shoes, etc. through the e-mail club's news. This has been one of my greatest resources for the links that are posted on my Web site.

In addition to Internet offers, this club can alert its members to local manager specials, clearances, and even regular weekly sales. Hey, even the Coupon Queen misses a good deal in the store once in a while! When someone goes to Wal-Mart and discovers they have a cart of Vaseline lotion marked down to $1, and you have a $1 coupon off any size Vaseline lotion, they alert the point of contact and she "smears" the word. If you're going to that store anyway, you can look for the good deal.

Of course you'll want to keep things in balance; it's not worth driving all over town to get one or two bargains. However, it is good to know about the values, and then you can decide if it is worth a trip (especially if you're going to the store anyway).

One word of caution: There is no need to exchange any money in this club; the e-mail account is free, and everything about this club should be free of charge to its members in order to remain legal.

While you're on the Internet, go to my Web site at *www.elliekay.com* and sign up for coolsavings. It is similar to the e-mail club I have described in this section, but it is on a national level and expands beyond the grocery store to include entertainment and department stores.

Legal Coupon Books

The rule of thumb is that you should never pay money for *manufacturer's* coupons because there is an 85 percent chance (or greater) that this is illegal. However, the local coupon book is an exception. These are commonly known as "entertainment books" and are used primarily as fund-raisers for organizations. They include coupons for free food or merchandize or reduced-price services, admissions, and other values. They are usually worth the price you pay for them (anywhere from $25 to $35 dollars per book) and they usually last for about a year. Discounts at restaurants, for haircuts, oil changes, and even reduced-price admissions to theaters and museums make this a worthwhile purchase. The fact that you are helping the nonprofit organization raise funds is a bonus.

If you visit a certain area often, or you are about to move, you can check the availability of these books in the new area by visiting my Web site at *www.elliekay.com* and linking on to *www.entertainment.com*. Or write Entertainment Books, 605 E. Robinson St., Suite 135, Orlando, Florida 32801; phone (407) 425-0057 or e-mail them at *askus@entertainment.com*. These books are also a good way to raise money for your school or organization.

Fruits and Vegetables

Whether you live in New York City or Alamogordo, New Mexico, you can save money on fruits and vegetables the way your grandma did. Cathy Zuidema from Wallaceburg, Ontario, Canada, wrote me this time-honored tip: "Make friends with the veggie/fruit man at your grocery store or produce market. I get tomatoes, carrots, bananas, and fruit of all kinds for less than half price."

The vegetables that Cathy's "Veggie-Fruit Man" throws out often have only a slight bruise or other minor defect. Look at the rejects as they are sorting vegetables and ask to buy them at a substantially lower price. It's so easy to cut a bad spot out of a green pepper when you're making the salad, or to discard the bruise in an apple when you make a pie.

If you live near a wholesale produce supplier, you can also ask to go through their rejected vegetables, which are probably in better shape than the discards in the grocery store because a wholesaler has to consider additional distribution time and handling when sorting their vegetables. One woman got enough strawberries from a wholesaler to make jam for her entire Christmas list—the regular price in a grocery store would have been over $100!

SHARE

SHARE is an acronym for the Self-Help and Resource Exchange. This national program is probably already in your neighborhood distributing food and sponsored by a network of churches, unions, community centers, and other volunteer-oriented organizations.

SHARE does not require a regular commitment, membership dues, or time commitments. Basically the way this program works is that you donate two hours of community service per month and sign up for the program one month in advance. Sign-ups are conducted by a host organization that will give you a form to have signed to validate your volunteer community service (teaching Sunday school, Girl Scouts, cleaning a widow's garage, etc.).

You will buy a package of groceries worth anywhere from $40 to $45 (amounts vary) for $15 (this price could have gone up, too, so check with your local SHARE). They will usually accept this $15 in food stamps or cash. This is not a government program, so participants do not have to meet income requirements in order to participate. The SHARE program buys their food from wholesalers or from growers. You will then pick up your food at a *specific time and place* or forfeit your prepaid investment.

The contents of the SHARE package includes 15 items, including 6 to 10 pounds of meat, 4 to 7 pounds of fresh vegetables, and 2 to 4 pounds of fruit. SHARE buys only nutritious food and ensures that people with poor food-buying habits are getting at least some healthy food.

For information on the SHARE program nearest you, go to *www.worldshare.com,* or to start one, contact:

SHARE
1250 Delevan Dr.
San Diego, CA 92102
(610) 525–2200

Assorted Tips

Dial for Dollars If you like a particular item, check the package to see if the company has a toll-free customer number. By calling, you can often get coupons for that item. I've received "free" coupons and many cents-off ones too.

Just Buy a Handful If your recipe only calls for a few pieces of cauliflower or broccoli, don't waste money on an entire head—especially if your hubby is not inclined to eat those items. Pick up what you need from the salad bar and avoid waste.

No Substitutes, Please Don't waste money on egg-substitutes; make your own by simply using egg whites. Most of these pricey items have primarily egg whites, with dyes and thickeners added.

Mix Your Own Make your own flavored yogurt by purchasing the least expensive yogurt—plain—and mixing it with fresh fruits or preserves.

Don't Opt for Convenience Quick-cooking rice can cost twice as much. Buy the long-grain rice, cook a greater quantity than you need, and freeze what is leftover to use as needed. You can also add your own seasonings to noodles, rice, vegetables, and pasta to save on the prepackaged varieties. (You'll also consume less salt by doing this.)

Weigh Your Produce Not all five-pound bags of apples are created equal. They can vary by as much as half a pound, so weigh before you buy.

Be a Latecomer Ask your grocer about late day markdowns in the bakery, meat, dairy, and floral departments. Meats that are near their expiration date can easily be frozen and then used immediately after thawing.

Rain Checks ALWAYS Sometimes I'm grateful when they are out of an item, especially if my coupon has some time on it before it expires. I can usually request a higher quantity on my rain check and have time to collect more coupons for that item while I wait for it to be restocked. I get free items all the time this way.

Share Just a friendly reminder: You don't shop for what you *need* in a store but for what is a good value. Meaning the item is on sale and you have a coupon so you pay the lowest price possible and have the item on hand when you need it. This also means you have extra to share with those in need.

How to Save on Cars

Why Buy?

One of the first things we need to ask ourselves before we buy any car is "Why am I buying it?" Are you tired of your present car? Can the car you have be repaired without major expense? How many miles do you have left on your present car? If you have a loan, how much do you still owe the bank on it? Do you really *need* a new car? Or is it just something you *want*? The "new-car bug" is a contagious disease in our country today, and when it bites you, you'll think your old car is falling apart.

> The least expensive car you can own is usually the "paid for" car you're driving right now.

The same questions apply to the genuine need for a second car. Could the two of you get by with one car? Perhaps you could car pool or one of you could ride your bike or take the bus to work.

Remember, the least expensive car you can own is usually the "paid for" car you're driving right now.

Used Doesn't Mean Abused

The average depreciation of a new car during the first year can be up to 31 percent of the price you paid for it. Incredible! With most new cars, you lose $5,000 as soon as you drive it off the showroom floor. Let someone else own it for that expensive year! Consider the purchase of a late model, low-mileage, mechanically sound, well-maintained used car. Take the car to a reliable mechanic and pay him to look it over. If at all possible, try to talk to the previous owner of the used car before you buy it—most of these folks will be honest. Be leery of repainted portions of the car—it usually indicates an accident. Look carefully under the car for rust. Once a car starts to rust, there's no turning back. Avoid buying a car from anyone who smokes. Cigarette smoke damages seals, glue, and upholstery. You may be willing to accept *minor*, not major, repairs on a vehicle if it will substantially reduce the price. Be prepared to pay for these repairs, adding them to the cost of the car. Negotiate for a 100 percent short-term guarantee, if possible, from the seller (at least one week). This guarantee should apply to dealers and individuals. After you drive the car for the first week, you'll find 90 percent of the problems you bought.

Blue Book

A trustworthy resource found in most car dealerships is the handy-dandy blue book. This is the book your bank officer also keeps handy. It lists the wholesale and retail value of a used car. The price is affected by mileage, wear and tear on the vehicle, and mechanical reliability—among other factors. You can also check the blue book value on the Internet at *www.edmunds.com*. It's better to secure a loan from your personal bank—negotiating and shopping for the best price. Know the blue book value of the vehicle and negotiate with the dealership as if you were a cash buyer—you won't be using their banks anyway. Try never to pay more than $100 over the wholesale value.

Trade-Ins

Try to sell your current car privately rather than trade it in. Detail it yourself—washing and waxing it to a glorious shine. As you clean and scrub, think of all the extra money you'll make with this minimum effort—it's surprising! Put an ad in your local paper, and another one up on the bulletin board at work, and tell your friends you're selling your car. If you trade in your vehicle to a car dealership, you'll get significantly less for it. It doesn't matter how much the salesman "says" he's giving you on the trade. They'll often inflate the value of the trade-in, and then figure the inflated amount in the negotiated price on the vehicle you purchase. It's not illegal but a card shuffle to get you to buy the vehicle.

When You Need New

Let's say your rich Uncle Harry has died, and you are his only heir. The only stipulation is that you *must* buy a new car in order to collect the millions waiting for you at the bank. If you must buy new, then try to avoid buying the newest, latest, greatest model—as soon as it comes out. Instead, buy an end-of-the-year clearance model, a demonstrator model, or a rental car. December and January are the best times to get these bargains, because that's when dealerships experience their lowest annual sales. Buy a cheaper model of the same vehicle rather than the luxury model. Buy the smallest car you can buy that will still fit your needs.

Leasing a Car

The only way to spend more on a car than buying it new is to lease a vehicle. Leasing a car is the most expensive means of driving a vehicle. The only exceptions are if you use it for business, anticipate extremely high mileage, or there is a substantial tax savings. If the only way you can drive the car you want is to lease it, then pass on it. There's a less expensive car for you that will still meet your needs.

Maintaining Your Car

Proper maintenance will improve your gas mileage and extend the life of your car by two or three years. How many of us know people who blew out the engine of a perfectly good car by ignoring the red light or forgetting to add oil? These kinds of mistakes are just too costly.

Maintenance Checklist

Weekly: Check the radiator fluid and the air in your tires; the wrong amount of air wastes fuel and accelerates tire wear.

Every other refueling: Check the engine oil level. Splurge on quality motor oil; it extends the life of the motor and increases miles per gallon.

Monthly: Check the battery's power indicator and cable connections for tightness and corrosion. Check transmission and brake fluids, the air filter, belts, and hoses. Replace these if they are worn, brittle, or soft.

As needed: Pay attention to warning lights.

Saving on Quick-Stop Oil Changes

Go to my Web site at *www.elliekay.com* and click on *www.valpak.com* or *www.hotcoupons.com* for a list of local garages that offer discounts and coupons. Some shops offer one free oil change when you buy ten, or other types of frequent-buyer programs. Sometimes you can use coupons on the oil changes you purchase.

Locating a Trustworthy Mechanic

You'll need a good mechanic as your advisor when you're considering a purchase and also when you service your present car. The best time to find a mechanic is before you need one. Ask your friends, neighbors, or co-workers for a reference. A mechanic's reputation—good or bad—usually follows him closely. To find an above-average mechanic in your area, go to *www.cartalk.com,* then select "Search the Site" and go to the alphabetical listing under "Mechanic Database." You can enter your zip code to start looking for a good mechanic in your area. Personal references are still (and probably always will be) the best way to find a reliable, honest, and less expensive mechanic.

How to Save on Furniture and Appliances

As you begin setting up your home—especially if you are buying a house—you need to be prepared for the additional costs of any appliances, furniture, or other home and yard necessities you will need to purchase now or replace in the future.

Plan Ahead

To save the most on furniture and appliances, you should prepare for these purchases *before* you need to make them. Set aside an emergency fund with as little as 1 percent of your monthly income—building up the fund to a healthy amount. When you need to replace something, you'll have the cash and won't spend more by using credit. Remember the old saying: "People don't *plan* to fail with their finances, they just fail to plan ahead!"

Taking Inventory

There are three questions that you need to ask yourself when you are considering major purchases:

1. "Do I need it?"
2. "Can I afford it?"
3. "How am I going to pay for it?"

Much of what we think we *need* is simply what we *want*. Do you really need all those little appliances that take up so much room and perform such a limited function? Go to garage sales, and you'll see all the stuff folks can do without. There you can buy your juicer, dehydrator, pasta maker, bagel baker, jerky jerker, taffy puller, and . . . well, I think you get the idea.

Evaluate your genuine furniture needs as well. Can you re-cover that couch with fabric from a wholesaler? Can you buy a slipcover for that chair? Does your mom have a piece of furniture or an appliance you could use sitting in her storage shed?

After you've taken inventory, write down your dream list and take it to a furniture or appliance store. The "sticker shock," or the price of the item you just can't live without, may force you to reassess your needs. Even if your fantasy furniture is marked down 50 percent or more, if you have to finance it, you may want to reconsider. You should never buy anything on credit without taking a look at the total price you'll end up paying for the purchase. The "steal" of a loveseat that costs only $500 will end up costing you an amazing $1,200 after several years on a low-payment, high-interest-rate schedule. If you're buying several pieces of furniture, you could accumulate $10,000 in credit card debt for furniture alone. By making only the minimum payment on that loan, at 18 to 22 percent interest, it will take you more than 33 years and $26,000 to pay it off! Count the cost before you buy to avoid the endless cycle of debt.

All right, you've assessed the amount of cash you have available and the maximum amount you can pay for the furniture or appliances you need. Now what?

Exploring the Internet

First, visit your local furniture or appliance store and write down the model numbers and brand names of the items you like. Now you're set up to do some profitable searches on the Internet. Often the brochures offered at these stores will have a Web site for the manufacturer. If they don't, you can either use a search engine to find the Web address or try typing *www.(manufacturer's name).com*. For example, *www.broyhillfurniture.com*. Once you have located the manufacturer's site, look for an outlet store link. Search for the price (including shipping and handling), availability, and delivery time of the item you want. Then print out those prices and take them back to your local store to give them an opportunity to match the competition's price. Another option is to explore the site and request a list of all the distributors of the brand-name furniture within a 100-mile radius. Printing the price list and making a few calls to the stores in your area could save you as much as 50 percent on your choices. When you call the local stores for a price check, don't forget to ask them if they can beat the deal you have by throwing in free delivery, a free fabric guard treatment, or any other freebie. So often these items are yours for the asking.

> **Never buy anything on credit without taking a look at the total price you'll end up paying.**

Model Homes

This is a creative approach that works best in larger towns or cities that are experiencing a new-home building boom. Call the local builders, especially those that have model homes, and ask the design manager how they liquidate the furniture and appliances in their model homes when they've sold the last home in the tract. Rather than going to the expense of using a liquidation firm to rid themselves of this excess, they are often willing to sell to individuals. Granted it would be easier to sell the contents to a wholesaler, but often you can pick up some beautiful pieces if your timing is right.

You will need to pay cash or by check (versus credit) for these items, so be prepared before you make an offer. Keep in mind also that furniture in model homes is usually much smaller than the furniture you would normally buy. Designers will place a double bed in the master bedroom rather than a queen-size in order to create the appearance of more space. The daybeds in these homes will usually accommodate a child not an adult, and the dining room sets may only have two to four chairs. Nonetheless, while these pieces are officially "used," they have only been used for demonstration and have not experienced the usual wear and tear of most furniture.

Secondhand Stores, Garage Sales, and Classifieds

The virtues and how-to's of finding quality vintage furniture and great appliances at secondhand stores, garage sales, and through the newspaper were well covered in *Shop, Save, and Share*. If you have some serious furniture and appliance shopping to do and don't already own this book, you might want to purchase it or check it out from the library. After twelve thousand loads of laundry, we still have the Maytag washer and dryer we bought *used* twelve years ago. We've only replaced a timing chain and another part damaged in a move—but the five hundred dollars we invested in them was money well spent.

Store Displays

Appliances that are removed from the box and used as store displays usually sell at discounted rates. By buying a store display and taking advantage of the reduced price and/or a rebate, you can save major dollars. The warranty is usually the same as any other new appliance in a box. Call around to your local dealers and ask for these values.

Consumer Buying Guide

Go to your library, or consider purchasing a current *Consumer Buying Guide* on the appliance or furniture you need. Rely on their extensive research on the most reliable models. If you are buying used, get back issues of *Consumer Buying Guide* to determine the best values in years past. ProQuest is a research program available on most library computers. They have access to over 1,200 periodicals and journals and make this information readily available.

The *Consumer Buying Guide* will list price ranges, reliability, and other comparisons of different models. If you do your homework before you shop, you'll know what features you need and the prices of the item you're shopping for.

Buying New

With your handy-dandy *Consumer Buying Guide,* shop the sales at each furniture or appliance store. Compare warranties, delivery charges, and features. Avoid the deluxe models—they have too many extra bells and whistles. You don't need them. We bought a small freezer and saved 35 percent by eliminating two unnecessary features. We decided we had enough noise at our house without the new freezer adding to the din.

Look at discontinued pieces of furniture and last year's models. Shop wholesale stores, and take your time. The more you look and watch the advertisements for sales, the more satisfied you'll be with your purchase. Ask the salesperson when the item might go on sale. If you just missed a sale by a couple of weeks, ask the manager for the previous sale price. Often you "have not because you ask not."

Manufacturer's Extended Warranty

Don't waste precious dollars on these extended warranties; instead, use a credit card that will automatically double the manufacturer's warranty, and then pay off the balance the very next month.

How to Save Money on Clothing

Newlyweds often spend more money than they realize on clothing—a $30 pair of jeans here, a $40 name-brand sweater there—and soon you have shot your monthly budget and added financial stress to your marriage.

There's nothing wrong with shopping at name-brand stores, and there's certainly nothing wrong with quality. My closet is full of name-brand clothing paid for by a dime on the dollar—or less. Still my wardrobe consists of quality clothing to be worn to spouse's functions, receptions, dinners, dances, formals, seminars, and even the local gym!

You can save 30 to 90 percent on clothing without sacrificing quality or style. The tips that follow will help you dress for less.

> You can save 30 to 90 percent on clothing without sacrificing quality or style.

New Versus Used Clothing

The most obvious way to save money on clothing is to buy it used. Some people are squeamish about germs or think used clothing is dirty. If you are one of these, wash it in hot (120°) water, and you'll get rid of any germs or dirt. Do you take your own sheets to hotels or use theirs? Do you ever try on clothing at a department store, even though someone probably tried it on before you?

Some people like the feel of new. Well, if I walked to my closet now, I couldn't tell you which clothes I'd purchased new and which were acquired used. They look the same. Who hasn't bought a brand-new article of clothing that puckered or ran after the first couple of washes? Buying clothing new does not guarantee it will wash or wear well. There is room for new clothes in a bargain hunter's closet, and I have quite a few. We'll look at buying new after we've finished looking at buying used.

Thrift Shops Versus Garage Sales

Finding quality bargains by shopping at garage sales is the cheapest way to buy clothing. However, if garage sales aren't your thing, thrift shops are an excellent alternative. Thrift shops may charge higher prices than garage sales, but they also have a greater selection. Also, most thrift shops have a place to try on clothing, so you can better determine fit and style. Some thrift shops have specials—half-price days or buy one/get one free days, among others. Call ahead of time to find out what their specials are.

Consignment Shops

These shops have the greatest selection but the most expensive prices for used clothing. They are often twice as high as a thrift shop (making them four times as high as a garage sale). However, their prices on formal attire and business clothing are hard to beat. If you develop a friendship with the storeowner, he or she can help you find the kind of clothing you need most. Some shops even keep a card file that lists your size and the style and color of clothing you are looking for.

Some people are squeamish about used clothing. Do you take your own sheets to a hotel?

Before You Shop for New Clothes

Look through your closet and take inventory of your present wardrobe. Some of the clothes that you haven't been getting enough use of may simply need to be altered, repaired, or dry-cleaned—thereby saving you a lot of money over buying something new. When you inventory your wardrobe, make note of the items you need most and their sizes. Take care of the clothes you have, paying special attention to the care instructions on the label. Use Woolite for sweaters and lay them out to dry. Use a coin-operated dry-cleaning machine or a dry-cleaning product you can use in your dryer instead of commercial cleaners to save 75 percent on dry cleaning.

Change out of church clothes or business clothes before lounging around the house to save wear and tear on your most expensive clothes. Consider buying classic, long-lasting styles rather than fads.

Perhaps the most important decision you can make when it comes to buying new clothes is never to buy on credit. You only dig a deeper hole and create more financial stress.

In Season/Out of Season

If you buy clothing before the season begins or in season, you'll probably *pay* top dollar. If you buy your clothes at end-of-the season clearance sales, you'll *save* top dollar. Try to buy quality clothing; check the seams, zippers, buttons, and fabric weight before you buy. In men's suits, stick with conservative styles and dark colors. Select wool or wool blends to extend the life of the suit and increase the wearing opportunity. Always hang up suits after wear, and air them out before putting them in the closet—it helps to minimize dry-cleaning costs. Before you store your clothes for the season, make sure they are clean. This prevents permanent stains and ensures their usefulness for the next season.

Discount Outlets

There is a trend in America for the discount outlet mall; you'll find one in every large city and throughout American suburbia. Watch these outlets carefully. Just because they are billed as bargain outlets does not mean they are bargain stores. I don't consider paying $75 for a $95 casual shirt saving money. The way I see it, that's *spending* money. When you happen upon a *real* outlet, though, you've got it made! These outlets offer values that range from 40 percent to 95 percent off retail prices. Look carefully for damaged zippers, etc., and consider each piece and its price. I've found some truly awesome outlet stores that rival the prices found at garage sales.

In Tuscaloosa, Alabama, I gave a seminar and had time to visit the Goody's Clearance Outlet. Most of the things were 75 percent off the lowest ticketed price. Of course, there was a size three hanging next to a size twenty-two, and the entire outlet was the size of a regular Wal-Mart store. In other words, some of these places are tough to "conquer." Undaunted, the pioneer blood that runs through these veins was up for the challenge. It took me three hours. But when I was finished I'd bought sixty articles of new clothing—or $350 dollars worth—for $52. Now *that's* what I call saving money!

CHAPTER 10

From "Love Shack" to "Beautiful Home"

How to Decorate Your Home Without Breaking the Bank, or Your Nails

From the time I was old enough to hold a crayon and find a white wall, I've been the creative type. My parents' home was filled with my works of art—on toilet seat lids, on the car dashboard, all over the television screen. As my mom scrubbed purple crayon off the green countertop, she'd simply say, "Ellie's been here!" As I grew older I turned this self-proclaimed "talent" into a profit-making business.

Long before there were "Furbys" I made critters for sale (fake fur fabric and plastic eyeballs). I coaxed unsuspecting neighbors and innocent bystanders into buying these hair creations and earned enough money to pay my way to summer camp. Since my dad was a building contractor, our toys consisted of things like empty refrigerator boxes and tons of

flat Styrofoam. Long before "The Muppets," I created puppet shows with these simple resources. And I learned some handy new tricks about crafting too.

Did you know that when you use your dad's blue spray paint on a Styrofoam frog, the frog will melt like the Wicked Witch in *The Wizard of Oz*? Did you also know that when said frog is on your dad's immaculate garage floor and it melts, it will leave bright blue paint in the shape of an amphibian—forever? Furthermore, did you know that when most dads discover the remnants of a blue amphibian on his otherwise immaculate garage floor that he begins to resemble that blue amphibian but with fangs?

Yes, I learned all these things and more. But there's one thing my parents didn't teach me about my creations. They withheld this information with smiles, and reactions such as "Wow, Ellie! How did you manage to glue all those split peas onto a yellow necktie?" Or my mom would say, "Ellie, I *never* would have thought to make a mama worm and her babies out of clay and use the rhinestones from Grandma Laudeman's antique jewelry for eyes!" (My mom still has the worms along with a flower vase with handles so big that they overwhelm the vase and a hole so small you couldn't poke even a single stem down into it.)

You see, long before there was self-esteem education, my parents knew that squelching the creativity of a loving and giving little girl would also squash her self-worth. So—I made 117 woven potholders for Mrs. Brewer, my third-grade teacher. Ellie, The Mad Creationist, fashioned a lopsided clay vase for my next-door neighbor, Mrs. Cooperman—and looked for it on display every time I went to her house to visit her poodle. (No wonder she asked my mom to call when I was on my way over to her house.) My parents' kindness to me was an *extreme* disservice to the rest of the neighborhood, who were laden with lopsided loot.

For most of my life I have been surrounded by "Creative Co-Dependents" like my parents. My husband now confesses that he was guilty of this type of enabling behavior in the first year of our marriage. He made the grave mistake of buying his new bride a $98 Singer sewing machine—and I went to town. I mean, I made multi-tiered bedspreads for our bedrooms (each side of the spread was a different length). I fashioned pillows for our living room, and when they didn't turn out exactly as planned, I affectionately called them "Patchwork Pillows." They had so many seams that the squadron commander's wife, who came to welcome us to our new base, said, "Oh my, I love quilting too" as she admired my work (another co-dependent).

I'll never forget the day when I was confronted with the truth. I'd just made some lovely ruffled curtains for Bob's grandma, Nana. She was a feisty seventy-year-old woman who ran an auto repair shop most of her life and cut people little slack. She spoke her mind first and never gave her words a second thought.

We drove 150 miles to her house in the San Fernando Valley of California with this love offering for her kitchen window. She had no curtains, and people could see right in, so I made her some gingham swags and bought a rod to hang them on. Much to my horror, when we got them on the rod, I noticed that I'd sewn the ruffles on *inside out!*

Bob regressed into his typical pattern, consoling his young bride: "Beloved, I don't think Nana"—he lowered his voice as she was in the next room—"will even notice; she can't see as well as she used to. I'm sure she'll love the thought."

As Nana entered the room, Bob seemed to be in a hurry to get out the door: "Well, we'd better get over to the restaurant for lunch. Come on, Nana, let's get in the car."

The elderly woman grabbed her purse and her sweater, and much to Bob's delight, headed for the door. As we exited the kitchen, Bob locked her door and breathed a sigh of relief. Just then Nana turned to me and said, "Why in the heck would you sew a ruffle inside out on a curtain and actually give it to someone as a present?"

The truth was out. The illusion was over. I was and forever would be—creatively challenged.

Life has a funny way of coming full circle. Now I have a little girl who crochets multi-colored baby caps and is constantly "saving" treasures for her craft projects. When she gave Bob a picture frame made of Popsicle sticks, he exclaimed, "Oh, how beautiful! I'll put it on my desk at work!" In fact, I don't even have to call him before Bethany and I bring brownies to the office—he keeps her work of art on his desk all the time.

Now, you might think a chapter on decorating tips would be totally out of line for a woman like me. I want to set the record straight on one minor issue: I may not be able to *create* home décor very well, but I sure know tasteful décor when I see it. I've been told by my parents, my husband, Mrs. Cooperman, and others that I have a beautifully decorated home. So you can trust me when it comes to decorating your home with inexpensive and simple ideas.

Bob, who was standing over my shoulder as I wrote the above paragraph, said that integrity dictates that I inform you that most of the following tips came from Wendy Wendler (*yes,* that *is* her real name). Wendy owns and operates an interior decorating company called "Wendy Wendler's Wonderworks" (we just call her WWW for short). She helps scores of people decorate on a budget, and she can even help the creatively challenged. Here are a few of her favorite tips:

Decorating Basics

As a new bride part of the fun of setting up housekeeping is in discovering how your tastes and your husband's will fit together. It may take some diplomacy on your part to get him to take down the hockey stick he loves to keep on the living room wall as "decoration." It might also take some creativity to incorporate some of the gifts you got as wedding presents. I'll never forget talking to a new bride whose husband's best friend was a cowboy. He gave them this gray, ball-shaped object that sat on an ugly concrete stand. When she opened the gift, she said, "Oh my, I've never seen anything like this! Um . . . what is it?"

To which the cowboy replied, "Well, that there's a gen-u-ine hairball—it comes from a cow lickin' his skin and grows inside the critter."

There's no requirement to use all your wedding gifts to decorate your home—especially if you don't have a cowboy motif as in our previous story. On the other hand, if your sweet, dear grandma made you some crocheted pillows, and she will visit your home, keep them in a nearby closet to quickly pull out when she visits. Or leave them out all the time as a sentimental reminder of this woman who loves you and thought of you when she made them. Your home will be a combination of décor that combines the sentimental with the aesthetic.

Here are some super tips to keep in mind when decorating any room. Once my friend Wendy told me these ideas, I quickly redecorated our front living area, and it looks amazing! Truly. When Bob came home and saw the candles, pearls, draping curtains and lace, a big grin spread across his face as he said, "This is amazing, Ellie. I can't believe you did all of this in one afternoon." It kind of reminds me of when we were first married. Isn't he cute?

Less Is More

Keep the lines in the room clean and free of clutter. Hang pictures at an eye level of about 5' 7" on the average, but don't be afraid to put a picture over a mantle or tall piece of furniture to draw the eye upward—especially if it is the central piece of furniture in a room.

One Room at a Time

Nancy Larson, a home makeover consultant, said in *Lists to Live By* (by Alice Gray): "Complete one room at a time. This will encourage you to keep going. You will be better able to see results when an entire room is redone than if you do one or two small things in several rooms. This can be discouraging."

> **"Complete one room at a time. This will encourage you to keep going."**

Paint

Nancy Larson says that the cheapest way to decorate is with paint. A couple of coats of paint will amazingly transform the drabbest of rooms. You should paint the walls a different shade than the woodwork if you have painted woodwork. When Bob and I were first married, we lived in base housing, and once we checked with the housing authorities, we found they would allow us to paint—if when we moved out we repainted it the way it was when we moved in. So if you rent a house or an apartment, be sure to check with the owner or manager before you paint. Some property managers will even pay for the paint if you provide the labor.

Stick to a Theme

If there is a consistent color scheme throughout the house, it's a good idea to maintain that scheme. If different rooms have a theme, try to stick to that general idea. For example, a country home should say "country" throughout. The same applies to neoclassic, hunt club, Southwest, primitive country, traditional, contemporary, or any other theme.

If you must have variety in your home, and call your taste "eclectic," then keep each *room* to a general theme, if not the entire house. The experts say, for example, not to mix contemporary and country in the same room.

You might even want to have a theme based on a particular decorating piece. My friend Elizabeth Kramlinger has a beautiful home with a gorgeous wreath in *each room*. As you walk through her home, you naturally look for each room's unique wreath.

Back to the Basics

Choose neutral furniture that is basic in design and color so that you can change the look of the room inexpensively. If you only have to repaint or wallpaper and add different accessories to change the entire room, it is far less costly than buying new furniture, especially if your furniture is still serviceable. As Pat Veretto of *Frugal Living* says, "Paint and wallpaper create the shell—the aura of a room, from which the rest are pulled. They're the cheapest and most effective ways to totally change the look of a room."

Share Subscriptions/Model Homes

Some of the very best decorating ideas are found in decorating magazines, but these can become quite costly to subscribe to. If your local library doesn't carry the magazines you like, you may consider sharing the cost of a subscription with your favorite decorating buddy. You could also spend a fun afternoon visiting model homes and seeing how they use limited space creatively. It is a great way to get your creativity flowing. Keep in mind, as we mentioned before, that the furniture in model homes is often downsized.

Decorator for Hire

Most new brides can't afford an $80/hour consultation fee for a professional decorator. But you don't need a professional to get that sleek look. Most of the best decorators have learned their craft through the keen power of observation. There are plenty of television shows to pique your creativity, such as *Martha Stewart Living, Trading Spaces,* or *Room by Room.*

Yard Sales

Another option would be to call a friend whose house you admire, invite her over, and ask her for suggestions. Better yet, if you offer this creative friend some coffee and chocolate, she might go with you to yard sales or auctions. Go to a few of these gold mine areas together and ask her for ideas. Look for baskets, plant containers, accent shelves, picture frames, theme pieces, candles, and greenery. By viewing these items through visionary glasses, you can redecorate your home for pennies on the dollar.

When in Doubt, Check the Net

There are some great sites out there that offer ideas such as *www.decorating-your-home.com* and *www.marthastewart.com*. Or conduct a *google.com* search for the latest sites.

Candles

A well-placed candle with or without a holder adds texture, color, height, or variety to any grouping. Wendy uses them on the fireplace mantle (don't be afraid to be asymmetrical in the arrangement), coffee table, stairway, and bathroom.

Greenery

Greenery anywhere in a room exudes a great feeling of "home." You can choose real or artificial, according to how you feel about plants. Look for greenery as well as silk or dried flowers at garage sales, end of season closeouts, and farmers' markets.

- To add more height to a tall, focal piece of furniture, place a plant on top of it.
- An artificial fern on a top corner shelf in a bathroom or on a cupboard brightens the entire area.
- Place a ficus tree with white lights in a bare corner. It adds warmth and sophistication to any room.
- Dried flowers in a recycled basket or vase make for long-lasting, inexpensive decorations.

Great Borders

Most people don't bother with this simple yet smashing decorating accent because they don't know how to hang wallpaper borders. There are self-adhesive borders, but they are often pricey, and the selection is limited.

For customized borders, simply find high quality wrapping paper in your theme with medium- to large-sized patterns. Get clear contact paper and cut it in the width of the strip you need. Cut out the wrapping paper images and press them onto the sticky side of the contact paper and stick it on the wall.

If you hang it crooked, like some people we know, who will remain unnamed, then gently pull it off the wall and hang it over again. These work great, especially in bedrooms.

Stencils

Wendy says that people are often intimidated by stenciling, and they miss out on an inexpensive and customized look because of their unfounded fears. I told her that I once stenciled a lovely blue frog on my dad's garage floor, and she said that's not what she meant.

"Stenciling is just like finger-painting in the first grade, and it's a great way of sprucing up the ordinary." So says my behind-the-scenes decorator. I think I should host a television show. I'd be in front of the camera demonstrating the tips and getting the glory, while Wendy would be busily working behind the scenes getting paint underneath her fingernails!

You don't need expensive stencil paints to do a professional job. However, you *do* need a good stencil brush as well as acrylic and water-based paints. This makes for an easy "clean off and paint over" if your new puppy jumps on your arm while you're painting.

If you practice on leftover scrap wood, it will boost your confidence and you'll soon wonder why you didn't do this before. You could also try paint crayons, because they go on easily. The key is to keep the stencil secure and flat and use a minimal amount of paint. Just follow the directions on the stencils.

To select the right pattern and proper stencil placement on the wall, you'll need to decide first what effect you want to create. If you want to break up a big wall area, then a pattern at chair rail height (halfway up the wall) will say, "Minimize me." A smaller pattern at the top of a wall by the ceiling will draw the eye upward and say, "Maximize me."

To mark a chair rail, use a tape measure or yardstick and measure the height desired with tiny pencil lines around the entire area. Placing the stencil on the edge of the pencil mark will help keep the pattern straight and uniform. If your pattern calls for three or more colors, remember to allow space for the additional design to avoid a cramped look on your wall.

Curtain Shortcut

Wendy says, "You don't have to be able to sew curtains to have beautiful and elegant window treatments. The secret lies in the rod and the fabric." What a relief!

Select an attractive rod that will accent your choice of fabrics. You should actually match the fabric to the rod. So take a swatch of fabric with you when you shop.

Purchase some Fray-Check in the sewing notions area and run a bead of this glue-like substance over the unfinished edge of your fabric to prevent fraying. Simply drape the fabric over the rod in a spiral pattern to create a graceful effect. When I told Wendy I didn't understand what she meant, she said, "It means put the fabric round and round on the rod in loose folds." This makes the folds uniform on the rod for a valance-type effect straight across the top of the window. Then adjust the folds for uniformity and texture. You'll be surprised at how easily you can have a pretty effect for just pennies!

Designer Bookends

Get an ordinary square garden paver (a concrete block available in different sizes and shapes at a nursery or garden center) in the desired size (they usually cost around a dollar). Wrap it as you would a gift package with fabric to match your curtains. Iron the tucked ends to flatten the surface and then hot glue the ends to secure them. They are heavy enough to hold anyone's books—including my complete collection of *Martha Stewart Living*!

Wallpaper

Often wallpaper can transform a room in just a couple of hours' worth of work. Be sure you buy high quality paper, which may cost a little more—but it goes on the wall easier and will last longer than cheap paper. Think about the pattern and the amount of space you have available. You could make a small bathroom look bigger with light-colored paper and a pattern that is not busy. Or you could make that same bathroom seem darker and smaller with a navy print that has a large pattern.

You can even paper only one wall in a room to save on costs, or simply use a border at the top. If you paper the lower three to four feet of the wall, you could then add a wooden chair rail at the top edge. Paint the chair rail first, in the same color as your wall, a complimentary contrasting color, or a wood stain. This adds a sophisticated touch and is something that both you and your husband could work on together.

The main idea in frugal decorating is to remember that you don't have to keep up with the Joneses or the Trumps. Decorating is an extension of your unique personality. And by keeping a few simple guidelines in mind, you'll develop your own classy style. Larry Burkett, bestselling author and founder of Crown Financial Ministries, says, "The main problem we have in America isn't that we're investing or saving too much. The main problem is that we're spending too much on consumables" (*Money Matters* radio broadcast, February 23, 2000).

You can decorate your home with creative alternatives. If you commit to this sensible approach in your home, you'll soon find yourself turning the simple into the marvelous. A wooden country stroller found at a garage sale for three dollars could become a plant stand. Your dad's old fishing pole and net can carry the theme in your husband's study. If you're *very* creative, you might even find a place for a cardboard refrigerator box and some serviceable Styrofoam!

The Best for Last

I've saved the very best decorating tips for last. They are taken right out of the book of Proverbs: "By wisdom a house is built, and by understanding it is established; and by knowledge the rooms are filled with all precious and pleasant riches." When I was a young wife with little babies, I cross-stitched this verse and many others and framed them. We didn't have much money to invest in decorating our home. Many of my friends had sleek, sophisticated houses, while mine was done in "early garage sale" motif. Another mom, Julie Klassen, described it best when she said, "My house is done in Wall-to-Wall Toddler."

You don't have to keep up with the Joneses or the Trumps. Decorating is an extension of your unique personality.

But I've learned that filling my home with designer fruit arrangements—the fruits of the Spirit, like love, joy, and peace—are indeed priceless. If I present patience, kindness, and goodness to my family and friends who enter my home, I'll never have to redecorate. I've also learned that faithfulness and gentleness make for a better atmosphere than a demanding attitude.

Throughout the years we have been blessed financially, and we've been able to add some lovely framed art, antique clocks, and gorgeous floral swags to our walls. But I've never forgotten that first year of marriage and those early cross-stitched verses that I crafted as a young bride. Even though they may not be on the cutting edge of modern design trends, they adorn our walls still. They serve as reminders of the most pleasant and precious riches we possess.

CHAPTER 11

BURNT OFFERINGS AND OTHER SACRIFICES

How to Entertain Without Embarrassment

I was a fresh-faced, starry-eyed, raven-haired, alabaster-browed new bride, and my dreams of establishing my own home were full of romantic notions. I set up our modest little house with special touches. I had put up curtains and decorated with country cows, and I was so proud of how smart and fresh it looked. One day I wanted to impress my hubby and make his grandmother's chicken-and-egg-salad sandwiches. My cookbooks were not yet unpacked and were somewhere in boxes at my parents' house—and they were out of town.

I didn't want to call Bob's Nana and let her know what a ninny her grandson had married because I didn't even know how to boil an egg—so I did the next best thing. I called my high school girl friend and asked her. I should have remembered that she never cooked in school—we always ate pizza or KFC or Chinese or popcorn and Diet Coke. How could she know? But when stars are in your eyes, common sense is usually nowhere to be found. So I called Donna.

"Hi, Donna! I'm so glad you're home!" I was relieved to get her on the phone.

"How's *married* life, Ellie?" she asked, emphasizing my married status, since I was the first member of our gang to take the plunge.

"It's really sweet, Donna, and my house is soooo cute!" I was still feeling that warm, soft, rosy glow that came every time I remembered that I was now a married woman. But I also needed to get on to the practical side of life and get my husband's favorite food cooked.

But before I could ask Donna my question, she got on a roll, "I can't believe you're *married*, it just seems like yesterday we were there and you were getting *married*. I mean, it seems like I was just wearing my bridesmaid gown and you were in your lovely dress and you were getting *married*." Donna stopped for a breath.

"Uh, Donna?" I quickly interjected, "It seems like it was yesterday because it was just *last week*. But hey, I've got a question for you—how do you boil an egg?"

"How do you boil an egg?" Donna exclaimed with her typical lilting laugh. "You don't know how to boil an egg?"

I began to feel a little defensive, "Hey! I don't remember you ever boiling an egg in high school, so don't think you're the Galloping Gourmet or something!" I sighed, "So are you going to tell me how to boil an egg or are you just going to laugh at me?"

Donna's answer was simple: "Anyone knows that you just boil it until it floats!" I heard her doorbell ring in the background as she bubbled, "Hey, that's Rob; I've gotta run now!" She was gone before I could say, "Are you sure?"

So I got out a dozen eggs, put them in a large pot of water and started boiling them.

And they boiled.

And they boiled.

And they boiled.

And all the water boiled away.

But they never floated.

Do you know what happens to eggs when they boil for about seventy minutes and all the water boils out of the pot?

They explode.

So the first bit of advice you'll want to know when it comes to cooking is *Follow printed directions from an authoritative source. And never ask a girl friend for cooking tips unless her last name is Childs or Stewart.* Here are some quick ideas to get you organized and started in the great adventure of entertaining.

Home Preparation

You don't have to have a perfect, spotless house in order to have friends over for fun. On the other hand, it is important to have a home you can be proud of, and that will require a little extra effort. There is a difference between having an immaculate showplace and a sloppy pigsty—your goal should be to live comfortably in the middle. But when you're entertaining, there are simple shortcuts you can take to make your house have the appearance of a showplace (even if it's still fairly piggish in places).

> You don't have to have a perfect, spotless house in order to have friends over for fun.

Have a Plan Decide what rooms will need to be cleaned and straightened, and plan your time in advance. There are some basic cleaning and organizing strategies that can be done several days in advance, while the last-minute vacuuming will need to be done the day of the event. You'll want to get grocery shopping done in advance too—so plan a day for that. But we'll talk more about menu planning later.

Delegate This isn't just *your* home or *your* dinner party—divide and conquer. After you've planned the menu and household duties, share the work with your spouse.

Create an Atmosphere Think about the kind of atmosphere you'd like to create in your home— elegant, informal, homey, fun—and plan accordingly. Select background music that fits the desired mood. Plan your menu, seating arrangements, starting and ending times, invitations (if desired), and any arrangements for children, if necessary. Candles, potpourri, freshly baked bread, all these smells greatly enhance your home's atmosphere for entertaining.

Spot Clean If you are running short on time and still want to put the best face on your home, only clean those rooms that you know your guests will be in. The guest bathroom, kitchen, living room, and dining room should be your primary focus. Then be sure your spouse knows that the spare room, office, and your bedroom are off-limits for guests. In other words, make sure he doesn't take them on an unscheduled tour of your love shack when some rooms are a wreck.

Concentrate Energies If you are having a barbecue in the backyard, be sure your husband gets the lawn mowed and the backyard in shape, and don't bother spending as much time cleaning the den if you will likely not have guests back there. If you're going to be inside or just on the back patio for coffee later in the evening, there's no need to stress out over having the garden mulched or the hedges trimmed—they aren't likely to be noticed at night.

Burn Candles—One End Only! While you want to create a comfortable atmosphere, such as burning candles, you want to make sure you don't burn the candle at both ends. If you clean the house from top to bottom, plan a menu you can't cook without great difficulty, or invite more people than your home can comfortably accommodate, you will burn out on the idea of entertaining. This is the primary reason that so many people don't even have friends over for dinner anymore—their unrealistic expectations make the effort entirely too stressful.

Guest Preparation

This doesn't mean you're serving "guests" for your next dinner party, but you *are* serving your guests. You especially want your first few times of entertaining as a couple to be successful—so set yourself up to be winners. Start modestly by inviting those who love you no matter what your Honey Dijon Chicken tastes like or whether you forget to serve the main course in a serving dish instead of the frying pan! Keep it low-stress by inviting those who get along with each other. If you know of animosity between adult siblings, invite them at different times. Think about how the guests will interact with each other. Be sensitive to your guests, whether they are single or married. Don't invite your eligible bachelor brother and three single ladies—he may feel set up.

Do the Santa Claus thing with your spouse: "Making a list, checking it twice, gonna find out who's naughty and nice." You don't want to invite someone who goads your hubby just to get a rise out of him. Nor do you want him to invite "Belching Billy" to the same dinner party as your elegant Aunt Ellen. But remember: Start small. Keep the numbers to a minimum until you gain confidence and work through the learning curve of entertaining with your husband in your new home.

Start modestly by inviting those who love you no matter what.

Hospitality

Here's a short list on the basics of great hospitality.

Propriety Versus Hospitality There's a world of difference between propriety—proper etiquette—and hospitality. The first will make Miss Manners happy, while the second will make your guests feel comfortable. Of course, if you're entertaining your husband's boss and his very proper wife, then you'll need to lean toward the Miss Manners end of the spectrum.

Sensitivity The key to hospitality is being sensitive to your guests and their needs.

Formality If Mrs. General is used to a more formal event and seems to enjoy meals served in courses with place cards, then consider stretching beyond your normal entertaining spectrum for this "once in a blue moon" event. But if you're very uncomfortable with the expectations of guests of this kind, minimize how frequently you entertain them.

Informality On the other hand, if Mrs. General feels she gets enough of the proper protocol from all her "mandatory fun" functions and wants nothing more than to kick back and relax—accommodate her with a more casual evening.

Greetings At a minimum, whether your event is formal or informal, it's important to greet your guests at the door. Both of you don't have to be there (although that would be preferable), but at least one of you should greet your guests when they arrive and then walk them to the door when they depart.

Drinks/Smoking If you don't serve alcohol in your home, don't feel compelled to change that—there are plenty of parties where alcohol isn't served. The same applies to smoking in your non-smoking home. Provide a nice chair and ash tray on the porch or patio for guests who need an after-dinner cigarette. When your guests arrive, and you've taken their coats or purses, invite them to have a seat and offer them a beverage of some kind. At the dinner table, be sure their drinks are at least half-full and fill them as needed.

Introductions You may have some functions at your home, such as a baby shower or community coffee, where the attendees wear name tags. But most events will not include these. Be sure to study the guest list, writing those names down at least once, to help you remember those guests you do not know well. Then, as they arrive, take them into the main room and introduce them to at least one other person or couple before you take your leave. That's why it's best to have both spouses at the door, so one can escort and introduce each guest as they arrive. Remember that when any newcomer walks up to a circle, it is your responsibility to make sure they know or have been introduced to the other people in the circle.

Basic Manners Even if you're hosting a Hawaiian luau at your home, basic manners are always in style. Chew with your mouth closed, never talk with food in your mouth, use your napkin instead of your sleeve, and don't belch. No kidding. Three nights ago we had guests over from Bob's work, and a man introduced his fiancée as someone who could belch as good as any man. I was not charmed!

Utensils This may seem obvious, but be sure you use your utensils for their designed purpose. For example, knives should be used to cut meat or butter bread—not to shovel peas into your mouth. Forks—not your fingers—are used to hold meat in place while you cut it (the wrong method was also used at dinner the other night). Spoons are used to eat soup, not mashed potatoes. You get the idea.

Meal Preparation

There's no need for you to do this alone, and it's important for your husband to contribute in all areas of entertaining. It might even be that you've been blessed with a husband who cooks, and you will be the one who assists *him* as he performs the lion's share of the effort.

Be Thorough   Write out full menus in advance that include everything you will need from the actual food to any special serving or cooking accessories.

Make a List   After you've prepared the menu, make a grocery list of nonperishable items and buy them well in advance and at one time.

Simple Is Better   Don't try out a new dish on company. Sometimes the simplest dishes (and I'll give a few later in the chapter) are the best.

When any newcomer walks up to a circle, it is your responsibility to make sure they know or have been introduced to the other people in the circle.

Bake in Advance   I always bake everything that can freeze in advance—bread, muffins, rolls, cookies, or frozen desserts (recipes follow).

Get Fresh   Purchase perishable items within days of the event so they will be fresh.

Combine Cooking   Read all your recipes and pay special attention to cooking times and dishes that can be mixed early and baked later. My squash casserole (Bob's fave) can be mixed even the day before and placed in the refrigerator to be baked right before dinner. If you are choosing between two recipes (for example, two vegetable dishes), select the one that can be baked at the same temperature as the main course or another side dish. This way, you can share the oven, save time and expense, and serve all the items fresh from the oven.

Place Settings   Whether you're serving buffet style, on trays, or at the table, prepare your place settings ahead of time so they'll be all ready when guests arrive.

Get Help!   Set aside a few jobs for guests who offer to help. This will reduce your work and stress at the same time. Good jobs for guests are slicing bread or desserts, taking drink orders, and placing last-minute items on the table (such as butter, jams, salads, cheese, or garnish, etc.). But if guests don't offer, don't ask. Not everyone is comfortable enough or realizes it's polite to offer to help in the kitchen.

Kitchen Hints From Heloise

Now that we've gone over some basic necessities for entertaining well, here are some basics you may need to know in the kitchen. One of the best investments you can make is in the book *Hints From Heloise* (Perigee Books, 1989) because it is chock-full of super ideas and serves as a reference guide for everything from removing stains to organizing your home. Here's a sampling of her kitchen tips with a few of my own added:

Cook Meat Thoroughly This is important because meat carries bacteria. Wash all areas where meat was handled (chopping board, countertops, etc.) with hot, soapy water.

Fresh Platters Never put cooked meat on the same platter you've placed the uncooked meat on. For example, if your hubby takes the steaks out to the grill, he needs to bring the platter back to be washed or get another one to put the cooked meat on.

Use Plastic Not Wood Plastic cutting boards are safer than wooden ones because they don't harbor bacteria from foods the way wood does.

Onions Place the onion in the freezer fifteen minutes before chopping, and your eyes won't water.

Garlic Buy fresh garlic and peel all the cloves at one time, then put them in a small jar of sesame seed or safflower oil. It will stay good for up to six weeks in the fridge.

Allspice Add one-fourth teaspoon of allspice to simmering chicken or turkey stock to get the fragrance of cinnamon, cloves, and nutmeg. Add allspice to cream soups or sprinkle a pinch over citrus fruits.

Sour Cream Substitutes Place six ounces of cottage cheese with one teaspoon of lemon juice in a blender and blend until smooth. You can also substitute plain yogurt—but try substitutes in the recipe in advance. Don't try it out on guests!

Emergency Substitutions

- 1 oz. unsweetened chocolate = 3 T. cocoa + 1 T. butter
- 1 T. cornstarch (for thickening) = 2 T. flour
- 1 cup buttermilk = 1 cup yogurt or 1 cup milk + 1 tsp. lemon juice or vinegar (left to set for five minutes)
- 1 cup milk = $^1/_2$ cup evaporated milk + $^1/_2$ cup water
- 1 cup cake flour or pastry flour = 1 cup all-purpose flour, less 2 T.
- 1 tsp. baking powder = $^1/_4$ tsp. baking soda + $^1/_2$ tsp. cream of tartar
- 1 cup sugar = 1 cup honey (use $^1/_3$ cup less in recipe)
- 1 cup brown sugar = 1 cup granulated sugar
- 1 whole egg = 2 egg yolks
- 1 small fresh onion = 1 T. instant minced onion, rehydrated
- 1 tsp. dry mustard = 1 T. prepared mustard
- 1 clove garlic = $^1/_8$ tsp. garlic powder

Weights and Measures

- 3 tsp. = 1 T.
- 4 T. = $^1/_4$ cup
- 5 $^1/_3$ T. = $^1/_3$ cup
- 8 T. = $^1/_2$ cup
- 10 $^1/_3$ T. = $^2/_3$ cup
- 12 T. = $^3/_4$ cup
- 16 T. = 1 cup
- 1 cup = 8 fluid oz.

- 1 cup = $^1/_2$ pint
- 2 cups = 1 pint
- 4 cups = 1 quart
- 4 quarts = 1 gallon
- 8 quarts = 1 peck
- 4 pecks = 1 bushel

Simple Tried and True Favorites

When I have a speaking engagement or am a guest on a call-in radio program, people usually ask me what we eat in our home. Here are a few of our quick and easy favorites you may want to try.

Sample Menu #1

> Don't try out a new dish on company. Sometimes the simplest dishes are the best.

Banana Bread

2 $^1/_2$ cups flour
$^1/_2$ cup sugar
$^1/_2$ cup brown sugar
3 $^1/_2$ tsp. baking powder
1 tsp. salt
3 T. oil
$^1/_3$ cup milk
1 egg
1 cup nuts (optional)
1 $^1/_4$ cups banana (2–3 medium)

Mix all together for 30 seconds (by hand).
Pour into greased 9" loaf pan, or 2–3 1-lb. coffee tins. Bake for 65–70 minutes at 350 degrees. (Check with toothpick after 60 minutes.) Bake and freeze in advance.

Spaghetti Pie

2 cups of leftover "Whatever Ya Got" spaghetti sauce (recipe following) or canned spaghetti sauce with meat

12 oz. spaghetti

2 T. margarine

2 eggs, beaten

$1/4$ cup parmesan cheese (cheddar or mozzarella)

1 cup cottage cheese (sour cream, cream cheese, or yogurt)

1 cup grated cheese (your choice; I like cheddar or mozzarella)

Boil pasta and drain. Add margarine, eggs, and $1/4$ cup Parmesan cheese. Pat into the bottom of a greased deep-dish glass pie plate. Add cottage cheese to center of pie, pour sauce on top. (This casserole can be prepared ahead of time and refrigerated before baking.) Bake at 375 degrees for 35–40 minutes or until set. Sprinkle 1 cup grated cheese on top and bake for 5 minutes more. Delicious!

Whatever Ya Got Spaghetti Sauce

1 can or jar spaghetti sauce

small jar of picante sauce

$1/2$ to 1 cup wine (depending upon how many other ingredients you have)

1 can mushrooms (if ya got 'em)

1 package of spaghetti sauce mix

basil to taste

garlic powder to taste

1 can Rotel tomatoes (with peppers; mild or spicey)

1 can stewed tomatoes

1 can tomato sauce

Sauté onions and peppers in olive oil (if ya got 'em).

Brown ground beef (I brown 5 lbs. at a time and freeze in one-pound portions to have on hand).

Mix any and all of this together, adding spices according to taste. Simmer in a Crockpot on high for several hours. Use in Spaghetti Pie recipe above or simply serve over spaghetti with garlic bread and a green salad. Always a favorite!

Squash Casserole

    1 cup evaporated milk*

    2 cups cooked squash, smashed

    $1/2$ cup margarine*

    1 cup chopped onion

    1 cup shredded cheese*

    2 eggs*

    1 tsp. salt, pepper

    2 cups crackers*, crushed

Combine everything in 2-qt. dish sprayed with Pam. Cook uncovered at 375 degrees for 40 minutes.

*Low-fat versions of these food items may be substituted.

Grandma Laudeman's Apple Cake

    2 eggs

    2 cups sugar

    $1/2$ cup oil

    $1/2$ tsp. salt

    2 tsp. soda

    2 tsp. vanilla

    2 tsp. cinnamon

2 cups flour

4 cups peeled, chopped, raw apples

1 cup chopped nuts

Combine all ingredients and pour into a 9" x 13" pan. Bake for 1 hour at 350 degrees.

Icing (optional):

Mix until smooth:

$^1/_2$ stick butter

2 tsp. vanilla

1 $^1/_2$ cups confectioner's sugar

6 oz. cream cheese

Spread over cake while still warm. Sprinkle chopped nuts over icing, if desired.

Sample Menu #2

Pumpkin Bread

$^2/_3$ cup shortening

1 $^1/_2$ tsp. salt

2 $^2/_3$ cups sugar

$^1/_2$ tsp. baking powder

4 eggs

1 tsp. cinnamon

1 can (16 oz.) pumpkin

$^1/_2$ tsp. cloves

$^2/_3$ cup water

$^1/_4$ tsp. nutmeg

3 $^1/_3$ cups flour

$^1/_2$ tsp. pumpkin pie spice

$^2/_3$ cup chopped nuts (walnuts or pecans)

2 tsp. baking soda

Heat oven to 350 degrees. Grease two loaf pans (or 4 coffee cans). In large bowl, cream shortening and sugar until fluffy. Stir in eggs, pumpkin, and water. In another bowl, blend together flour, soda, salt, baking powder, and spices. Add to wet mixture. Stir in nuts.

Pour into loaf pans. Bake *about* 70 minutes or until wooden pick inserted in center comes out clean. Cool in pans for a few minutes, then remove to racks to finish cooling.

Chicken Spaghetti Casserole

6 chicken breasts

$^1/_2$ cup picante sauce (medium or mild, to taste)

1 small can green chilies (mild)

2 cans cream of chicken soup (cream of mushroom, or sour cream)

1 small can sliced black olives (optional)

$^1/_2$ medium sautéed onion (optional)

2 tsp. garlic powder

2 tsp. ground pepper (or, to taste)

2 cups grated cheese (your choice; I use cheddar)

16 oz. spaghetti

Stew chicken, de-bone and save broth. Boil spaghetti in broth and set aside while you mix together all other ingredients, including chicken. Drain spaghetti, saving 1 cup broth. Add spaghetti to other mixture and mix well, using extra broth (if needed) to make a creamy consistency, (should not be too soupy). This recipe will make two large casseroles; divide mixture into two greased 15" × 9" pans. You may want to make these ahead of time, refrigerating one for your guests and freezing the other to have on hand or to share with a neighbor. Bake at 350 degrees for 45 minutes or until bubbly.

Copper Pennies

> Peel and slice one pound of fresh carrots.
>
> Steam until somewhat soft (but not mushy).
>
> Transfer to saucepan with $1/2$ stick butter or margarine and $1/2$ cup of brown sugar.
>
> Simmer on low until sauce thickens (about 30 minutes).

Cake Mix Cookies

> 1 cake mix (any flavor you like)
>
> 2 eggs
>
> 2 T. oil
>
> $1/4$ cup water

Add only one or a mixture of $1/2$ cup each of any of the following:

> chocolate chips
>
> M&Ms
>
> chopped nuts
>
> raisins
>
> coconut
>
> Rice Krispies

Mix together, drop onto a greased cookie sheet. Bake at 375 degrees for 8–10 minutes. Makes two dozen very sturdy cookies.

Our favorite variations include spice cake mix w/raisins, party cake mix with candies, and yellow cake mix with M&Ms.

Cream Cheese Cookies

> 8 oz. cream cheese (light variety is fine)
> 1/2 stick margarine

Cream together and add 1 egg yolk and 1 tsp. almond or vanilla flavoring.

Add one dry cake mix. (Use white, chocolate or lemon; add 1/2 at a time).

This will be very stiff; beat by hand. Refrigerate for one half hour. Drop onto ungreased cookie sheets.

Bake at 375 degrees for 10 minutes.

These are pretty with nuts on top. Enjoy!

Sample Menu #3

Easy Olive Oil Chicken

> 4 frozen boneless, skinless chicken breasts (or half this for two)
> 4 T. olive oil
> 1 1/2 T. chicken bouillon granules
> water to cover chicken to about half their thickness (about 1 1/2 cups)

Pour olive oil, frozen chicken, and water into large frying pan, sprinkle with bouillon. Cover and cook over medium high heat for 20 minutes. Turn over and cook until water evaporates and chicken is cooked through—about 25 minutes more (replenish water sparingly, if needed). Brown chicken in olive oil, turning again to brown the other side. Serve with steamed broccoli, baked (i.e., microwaved) potatoes or Squash Casserole.

This is a handy recipe for those nights when you come home and realize you forgot to take something out of the freezer!

Almond-Orange Salad

> iceberg or romaine lettuce, shredded
> 1 cup celery, diced (if you have it)

1 can mandarin oranges, drained

1 small onion, cut into rings (red or white, or substitute green onions)

$^1/_4$ cup Caramelized Almonds (directions follow)

Sweet & Sour Dressing (recipe follows)

Easy Caramelized Almonds

The traditional way of carmelizing almonds (stirring constantly in a saucepan with sugar for what seems like hours) is tedious and time consuming. Here's an easier alternative method that is almost as tasty.

On a double thickness of foil, or a baking sheet, spread sliced almonds. Spray liberally with vegetable oil cooking spray (Pam) and sprinkle with granulated sugar. Bake at 350 degrees for 10–15 minutes until nuts are lightly browned.

Sweet & Sour Dressing

$^1/_4$ cup vegetable oil

2 T. vinegar

2 T. granulated sugar

$^1/_2$ tsp. salt

dash pepper

Combine all ingredients in a jar; shake well.

Cookies and Cream Dessert

1 pkg. Pecan Sandies cookies (or Oreos)

$^1/_2$ gallon praline pecan or butter pecan ice cream (or whatever flavor you like)

1 jar caramel sundae topping (or fudge topping, if you're using chocolate cookies)

Crush cookies and reserve about 2/3 cup of crumbs. Press crumbs into the bottom of a 13" × 9" pan. Allow ice cream to stand at room temperature until slightly softened. Spread ice cream over cookie crumb crust. Drizzle sundae topping over ice cream. Sprinkle reserved crumbs over the top. Cover with foil and freeze. A super-easy make-ahead dessert!

Game Dame Menu

Whatever Ya Got Chili
Add whatever ya got—or like—of the following:

> canned chili
> packaged chili spices
> garlic powder to taste
> chili powder to taste
> 1 can Rotel tomatoes (with peppers; mild or spicey)
> 1 can stewed tomatoes
> 1 can kidney beans or chili beans
> ground beef, browned
> jar picante sauce

Having friends over to watch the game? Prepare this chili in the morning and simmer in a Crockpot on low for 4–5 hours. Serve with homemade cornbread and veggies and dip.

Easy, Like Homemade, Cornbread

Use packaged cornbread mix, but add 1 tsp. sugar (per 6 servings). Follow directions for pan cornbread and add four pats of butter to the top of uncooked batter before baking. A yummy variation!

Pumpkin Roll

> 3 eggs
> $3/4$ cup flour
> 1 cup sugar

1 tsp. baking soda

²/₃ cup pumpkin

1 tsp. cinnamon

Mix together all ingredients. Grease a jellyroll pan liberally with Pam. Line with waxed paper and spray again. Pour batter into jellyroll pan and bake 15 minutes at 375 degrees.

Remove from oven and let cool 5 minutes.

Icing (prepare while cake is baking):

8 oz. cream cheese

4 T. butter

1 cup powdered sugar

1 tsp. vanilla

Whip ingredients all together with beaters, set aside.

Sprinkle a kitchen towel liberally with powdered sugar (so cake won't stick to the towel). Place the cake on this towel and sprinkle the top of the cake with powdered sugar as well. Roll the cake in the towel and let stand for 20 minutes.

Unroll and fill with cream cheese mixture.

Re-roll and refrigerate overnight. Or this can be made ahead and frozen.

CHAPTER 12

HOLLY DAZE

How to Agree on Holidays,

Establish Traditions, and

Preserve Memories

Samantha stormed into the house and slammed the door. "I don't know why I ever married a man whom I have *nothing* in common with!"

Her mom, who was sitting in the comfortable living room chair, looked up from her book and without batting an eyelash replied, "You didn't marry someone exactly like you, daughter, you married someone different, who completes you."

Tossing her long, honey-blond hair back, Samantha nervously chewed on the corner of a manicured nail. "But Bill is so argumentative, Mom! He wants us to go to HIS parents for Thanksgiving Day! I ALWAYS spend Thanksgiving with *our* family," she wailed.

Samantha's mom adjusted her glasses, peering over them at her daughter. "Welcome to

married life, my dear!" She wisely continued, "A good marriage isn't about never disagreeing, it's about working through difficult situations with give-and-take—even when it seems like you're the one giving more than taking."

Where to spend the holidays was one of the most volatile topics in Bill and Samantha's first year of marriage. But a lot of the tension could have been eliminated if this couple had taken the time to sit down and discuss the holidays long before the season arrived.

Let's face it, the old saying "You can please some of the people some of the time, but you can't please all of the people all of the time" is never more true than when it comes to where newlyweds are going to spend the holidays. When you add stepparents, siblings, and grandparents, you can become torn in so many directions that most of the joy of the holiday is torn away too. The goal is to come up with a plan that is acceptable to both spouses so that everyone comes out a winner, while realizing you won't completely satisfy extended family members.

An exercise that will help get the conversation started toward a win/win result is to get out a sheet of paper and write down each holiday that could possibly be spent outside your love nest.

Next, each of you list *individually* the ways you would like to spend each holiday. This column will likely be largely based on what your family traditions were like while you were growing up. Also list the feelings you have associated with the holiday. Finally, you will have to compromise with lots of understanding, using positive communication techniques to decide what you will do for each holiday as a couple.

Like Bill and Samantha, some of the questions you'll need to consider are *Do you want to simplify the season? Go to parties and be with people? Stay within a limited travel budget? Or spend the day in the comfort of your own home?*

Look at Samantha and Bill's sample list on page 180. Can you see why it led to a doozie of an argument?

Samantha was raised in a gentle southern family where it was commonly understood that holidays were celebrated in a formal manner, centered around tradition and family. Bill was raised by a single mom who had so much on her plate that she just let her boys have a day off on holidays to do whatever they wanted to do and relax. Bill didn't have to change his "tradition" to accommodate anyone during his bachelor days, so it came as something of a shock that his wife wanted to spoil his fun day off with a bunch of traveling, cooking, preparations, and endless running around. But this couple had two things going for them: (1) Samantha's mom's exhortation to her daughter to "work it out, and we'll support your decision" and (2) some basic communication skills that were put to good use.

This couple might be an extreme case, but if they can reach resolution with their diverse backgrounds, then so can you. By sitting down together and discussing the holiday topic, using the skills and guidelines we established in chapter 5 of this book, they were able to avoid future arguments on the same topic and put to rest any smoldering ashes left over from the last disagreement. As you can see from the final column in the chart, each side had to give and take in order to reach a consensus.

In their discussion, they took into account the fact that their background in celebrating holidays greatly impacted their expectation for such celebrations within their marriage. They also realized that the decisions they made in the "here and now" would affect their future children and the rest of their family. So they made their decisions based on what would maintain peace, create lasting and loving memories for their new family, and be an asset to their relationship. They also kept in mind the fact that any decision would not be set in stone but could be modified to meet their future real and felt needs, geographical location, and family situation.

You may know of other couples who continually battle with their parents and/or in-laws over these kinds of issues. What if you are a couple who engages in this kind of battle? Well, in the next chapter I'll address the specifics of how to go against the wishes of parents and yet somehow survive it. Another good resource, besides the ones I'll mention, is John Townsend and Henry Cloud's book *Boundaries* (Zondervan, 1992). But in the meantime, here's a plan to get you started on planning your holidays for this coming year and for many happy years to come.

Holiday Celebrations Worksheet—Year of _____

Holiday	Samantha	Bill	Compromise
Thanksgiving	1. Watch Macy's parade. 2. Lots of food, fine china, and dressy attire. 3. Traditional menu. 4. Spend entire day with extended family. 5. Each family member shares two things they are thankful for.	1. Sleep in late. 2. Camp out at home in grubbies. 3. Pizza or whatever. 4. Watch football games all afternoon. 5. Get to bed early after eating the leftover pizza.	1. Bill sleeps; Sam gets her cocoa and watches the parade. 2. Every other year they will have a traditional dinner at the relatives' house. The other year is spent at home with a turkey menu. 3. They share what they are thankful for. 4. Alternate Christmas/Thanksgiving with relatives (when within traveling distance).
Christmas	1. Christmas Eve church services. 2. Up at 6:00 A.M. to read Christmas story from the Bible. 3. Open presents one at a time, thanking between each one. 4. Formal dinner at Grandma's house. 5. Ice-skating in the afternoon. 6. Christmas caroling at night.	1. Open presents on Christmas Eve. 2. Sleep in late and wear pajamas most of the day. 3. Few presents, the holidays were downplayed. 4. Pizza or whatever, maybe tacos. 5. Watch football games and then take a nap. 6. No particular traditions, Christmas was just commercialism.	1. Go to services, when available, and open one gift on Christmas Eve 2. Bill sleeps in and they read the Bible story when he wakes up (by 10:00 A.M.). 3. Three gifts, opened one at a time. 4. They realized that the holiday can have the significance you give it. 5. Football in the afternoon and caroling at night (when possible).

Even without the differences of opinion as to how the holiday should be celebrated, holidays are notoriously stressful. A large part of that stress can be directly traced back to the financial stress of the season, unrealistic expectations, and over-commitment. Here are a few ideas that have worked well for our family that can help de-stress the holidays and at the same time get your creative juices flowing for how you can establish new traditions for your family.

Thanksgiving

Let's Talk Turkey

By using my method of grocery shopping (as found in my book *Shop, Save, and Share,* this is the best time of the year to stock up on baking supplies. The reason for these great bargains is that the loss leaders (items grocery stores sell at less than cost to get you to come into their store) and coupon values are best at this time of year. The more items you can bake and give as holiday gifts, the more money you can save. Almost everyone enjoys homemade goodies, so stock up during this season and save money on the next!

The largest expenditure for this holiday tends to be the meat. Think "turkey" at the beginning of the season and wait for the feeding frenzy to start in earnest about two weeks before this holiday. If you watch the sales, frequent buyer deals, and store coupons, you can get an amazing deal on your big bird. Last Thanksgiving, Albertson's had a buy one/get one free offer on their store brand turkeys. Their competitor, IGA, had a special for a store brand 12- to 15-pound turkey for $6 with the store coupon. Since Albertson's honors competitor's coupons, I was able to take the IGA coupon there and get the first turkey I bought for only $6. Since the buy one/get one free was a store special and not a coupon special, I got the second turkey free. So I got two 15-pound (always get the most meat in the weight range they offer) turkeys for only $6. I kept one and gave one to the Salvation Army, who was having a shortage on turkeys that year.

Thankful Traditions

Not every "savings" can be measured in dollars and cents. One of the things we emphasize in our family is the saving of *memories*. Our "Thankful Tree" was featured in a *Woman's Day* magazine one year. It took two photographers *eight* rolls of film and *four* hours to get *one* 3 x 5 photo in the magazine. Joshua was missing for one roll of film, and we didn't notice until we saw him making faces from *behind* the photographers.

The tip we shared in the magazine is how we stay in touch with family and friends during this holiday. On November 1 we make a Thankful Tree on poster board and put it on our wall or front door. The tree is bare because the leaves that we make out of construction paper have not yet been gathered. The leaves have the name of a friend or family member on them and a place for the person to write what they are thankful for. For example, "Uncle Steve is thankful for _____." But we put the tree up bare at the beginning of the season to teach the children how barren our lives are without the giving of thanks.

We make and send the leaves to friends and family around the world along with a self-addressed envelope. When these envelopes begin to come back, the children get excited as they take turns opening them. At dinner that night, we read the leaf and give thanks along with those who are thankful and put the leaf on our tree. By Thanksgiving Day, we have a tree full of thanks. We carefully save the leaves in an envelope marked by the year and keep them all in our Thanksgiving decoration box. Each year we read the leaves from past years.

We never know when this year's leaf might be someone's last, or which family might have a new leaf on next year's tree. So we give thanks.

Five Kernels of Corn

In the first year our Pilgrim Fathers came to America, there were periods of time when food was so scarce that the daily ration only consisted of five kernels of corn. In remembrance of these difficult circumstances upon which our nation was founded, we each get five pieces of unpopped popcorn and take turns passing around a basket. As we drop each kernel into the basket, we name five things that we are thankful for this year.

Christmas

Document Purchases

There's nothing like buying Christmas paper to wrap those presents early only to discover a month later that you have tons of paper you bought at the end-of-season clearance last year that you forgot about. Or you get a good deal on gifts for friends and then realize you bought those earlier in the year and forgot where you put them. To avoid the stress of forgetfulness, write down your purchases—and where they're located—on a piece of paper and tape it to next year's December calendar page.

Decorate Early

Decorate the weekend after Thanksgiving, and you'll save money. By organizing all the Christmas decorations, you'll discover which items you need and which ones you do not need. Then you can look for those lights that are on sale to replace the ones that didn't survive last year. You also will not duplicate items that you bought on clearance the previous year. With your home decorated early, you'll also be less inclined to impulse-buy holiday decorations, and you won't have the job of decorating on your "to-do" list.

Wrap As You Buy

Get this done as soon as the gift is purchased and you won't have to worry about hiding it! Be sure to add the gift tag when you wrap so you don't forget whom the gifts are for. You may want to keep a master gift list so you remember what you bought for whom.

Emergency Gift Closet

It's a good idea to have extra gifts on hand in case an unexpected guest turns up with a present in hand. These can appeal to a broad range of tastes, such as holiday music or classic holiday videos like *It's a Wonderful Life* or *White Christmas*. Other safe gifts include holiday fashion accessories—from cuff links to earrings to socks and scarves; everyone loves to show their holiday duds.

Christmas Stress Busters

"It's the most wonderful time of the year..." or so the song goes. Yet why do we suffer so much stress and insanity during this season? Christmas can be a major budget buster. It only takes a few short days to wipe out an entire year's worth of diligence.

> Think "Christmas" all year-round and shop the clearance aisles and loss leaders.

Thinking about the spirit of Christmas every day of the year helps during the hectic season. It reminds us to prepare throughout the year—thereby minimizing the stress of the holidays and the expense. Here are some pre-holiday tips.

Buy on December 26 Christmas paper, bows, cards, decorations, and nonperishable gifts. Think about those items that will store well and invest accordingly. One season I bought enough (incredibly cute) gift bags (at 90 percent off retail) to last five years! My entire bag investment was only $10.

Buy Year-round Try to think "Christmas" all year-round and shop the clearance aisles and loss leaders. These expenses are absorbed into our monthly budget, and we get the benefit of sales and clearance prices on gifts.

Photo Greeting Cards We have photos made in October and get the savings of an early-bird discount on photo greeting cards. If you try this your first year of marriage, it will be fun to see how your family changes as the years go by.

"Sending out Christmas Cards" is the holiday chore that tends to be procrastinated the most—and hangs over the heads of the procrastinators, thereby causing cumulative stress! Surprisingly, the "card" job can cause more consternation than buying gifts!

By writing an annual Christmas letter in the middle of November and addressing the envelopes before Thanksgiving, the cards can go out the day after Thanksgiving. You can save yourselves the stress of that task during the holidays and actually get those feel-good endorphins going because you're actually *ahead* of the game!

Bake Ahead of Time   Baked goods are the standard Kay family gift to neighbors. We try to get this baking done around the first of December and deliver these goods early. I make items that freeze well and can be baked in several portions. For example, the banana bread and pumpkin bread (recipes found in chapter eleven) are baked in coffee cans, and they freeze well. By making four coffee can loaves instead of two regular-size loaves, I have a quick gift as close as my freezer. Tie a pretty bow around it or some raffia, add a photo greeting card, and you have a yummy personalized gift.

Simplify   The reason we keep our gift giving simple is *not* because we're cheap. It's because we want to keep the focus on the Reason for the Season. Holiday mania detracts from the coming of the Christ Child as God's greatest gift to us.

Three Gifts   Part of the Kay Family Simplification Plan involves the number of gifts each of our children receive. This could also apply to each spouse, before the kids start coming along. I'll never forget one Christmas before we had children. Bob and I watched a little boy get so many gifts for Christmas that he got tired of opening them and quit. Sadly, he was so spoiled by his parents and grandparents that he had the mistaken notion that Christmas was all about him.

We limit the gifts to three per person, since that's how many gifts the wise men gave baby Jesus. We've decided—if it's good enough for the Christ child, it's good enough for us. The gifts are selected carefully, paying special attention to the recipient's tastes and our budget.

It Really Works!   Listen to what Sandy from Colorado writes about trying the "Kay Simplification Plan":

> I wanted to try your Christmas simplification plan with the three gifts but didn't know how our family would take it. But our finances really needed it. It seems like it takes forever to pay off the credit card bills from Christmas. We explained the idea to the kids, and they seemed to understand. They even made a game of trying to pick three simple gifts they really wanted.

Well, it worked beautifully! We had told the kids they might not get everything on their list, and we found clearance items, like you said, that weren't on the list that the kids liked even better than the things that were on the list. For the first time in seven years, we don't have credit bills to pay off from Christmas. The emphasis was on the reason for the season and we don't have the headaches of bills to pay. Why didn't we start this years ago? Thank you, Ellie Kay, for your work in this area.

> Sometimes the gift of time is the greatest gift of all during the holidays.

Sandy is so right when she asserts that it seems to take forever to pay credit card bills. The average American family takes until May of the following year to pay off Christmas debt. That doesn't leave much money left to save for vacations or to service other debt. Here are some ideas that will save time, money, and memories:

Sharing Christmas

Sometimes the gift of time is the greatest gift of all during the holidays. There are a number of ways you and your spouse can brighten the holidays of those around you and share the season. We like to visit nursing homes and just spend time with the residents, talking and sharing. If you know of an elderly relative, neighbor, or friend who rarely gets to decorate for the holidays, why not help them set up a tree and lights? Then after the season is over, help them put the decorations away.

One of the traditions on military bases is a holiday cookie drive. Last year we collected 10,000 dozen cookies and distributed them to police, firemen, and others who worked the holiday shift. You could take a basket of goodies to your local firefighters or police officers on duty. I know they would enjoy these treats on Christmas Eve! We even bake cookies for the mail carriers and sanitation workers and have for several years. We place these in easy to carry plastic bags and include a can of soda.

Start early in your marriage to include the tradition of sharing with others as you see their needs. Reaching out and thinking about someone else is one of the greatest joys you will find during the holiday season. When you do it as a couple, you are doubly blessed as you become a blessing to others!

Living Happily Ever After

Building for the Future

"Why, You Dirty, Rotten Varmint: I Said 'In-Laws' *NOT* 'Outlaws'!"

CHAPTER *13*

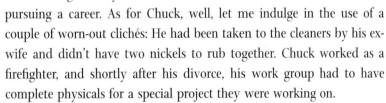

How to Get Along With Your Relatives

I love hearing how people met, fell in love, and got married. Every story is different, and every one is very special in its own way. Over half of the couples getting married these days have been married previously, and that was the case with our dear friends the Baxters.

Cynthia and Chuck had a short courtship and then eloped. They wouldn't necessarily recommend it—as a matter of fact, they're scared to death that their kids will follow in their footsteps. Short courtships sometimes make for short marriages, but not in this case.

When they met, both were in their twenties and each had a failed marriage under their belt. Cynthia had sworn off dating entirely, and she was content to live the rest of her life

pursuing a career. As for Chuck, well, let me indulge in the use of a couple of worn-out clichés: He had been taken to the cleaners by his ex-wife and didn't have two nickels to rub together. Chuck worked as a firefighter, and shortly after his divorce, his work group had to have complete physicals for a special project they were working on.

When the nurse approached Chuck and said, "We'll need some blood now," his co-workers immediately responded,

"He doesn't have any—his ex-wife took it all!"

But one day Chuck was introduced to Cynthia by a mutual friend, and they all went out together for dinner and dancing at a trendy restaurant on the West Coast. After dinner, Chuck found himself seated by Cynthia at the side of the dance floor, and they started talking.

Cynthia describes it dreamily: "It was like a scene from the movies, where the background fades and there's no one left in the room but the two of you. We talked for three hours solid, while our friends danced, ate, went out for coffee, and came back."

Chuck laughs, and adds, "Yeah, our friends knew there was something special going on. They kept coming back to our table, and out of our peripheral vision, we could see them sitting and staring at us with a look that said, 'What in the world is going on between them? They just met!' But we were pretty much oblivious to the rest of the world."

Chuck used to joke with Cynthia when they were together, "Baby, I'd marry you tomorrow!"

And much to his surprise, one day Cynthia responded with, "Okay. Do it! Marry me tomorrow."

So with two of his baffled co-workers as witnesses, Chuck married Cynthia in the small apartment of a friend (who happened to be a preacher on the weekends and a truck driver during the week)!

Fifteen years and a few kids later, they are still madly in love with each other.

But the Baxters' story got even better when they told us how Cynthia's parents took the news of the elopement. When Cynthia married the first time, right out of college, she had a massive, elaborate wedding in a big city cathedral. The reception was at a country club and the proud parents hired a band and had a full buffet for the guests.

So even though her parents liked Chuck, and knew the couple were likely going to get married, they responded strangely to the fact that there would be no gala affair this time around.

Cynthia said, "Chuck and I arrived at my parents' home and sat in their living room. I was nervously trying to figure out how to tell them, and decided I should just get on with it." She haphazardly ran her fingers through her hair and continued, "I said, 'Mom, Dad, Chuck and I eloped this weekend—we're married!' "

Cynthia paused and looked at Chuck as she recounted the story all these years later, "My mom has always been a bit high strung, and we like to say that she comes from a long line of overreactors."

She looked at Chuck and gave him a smile of resignation, then took a breath and continued, "When we told them, my mom stood up, screamed, and ran crying from the room to the back of the house."

Chuck took over. "I was amazed, but what was even more amazing was Cynthia's dad's reaction. He suddenly sat up straight in his chair, put his glasses on the bridge of his nose, and started playing tiddlywinks with his fingers."

"Then he told Chuck, 'Uh, this was rather unexpected. Uh, my wife isn't really upset. Uh, she's just venting a bit.' We could hear my mom's wails coming from the back of the house, and when Chuck looked at me, I could see that all the color had drained from his face and he was at a loss for words." Cynthia smiled wryly. "But I knew my family."

"So I looked over at my new husband and simply said, 'Welcome to the Duncan family!' "

Hopefully you had a better introduction to your family than Chuck did! Whether you have the perfect in-laws or difficult in-law relations, it's important to value family, establish healthy boundaries, and minimize conflict as you strive to live in peace with those who love the one you love.

Let's look briefly at those three areas and see how they fit into your marriage relationship and why they are so important.

Value the Family Blessing

The first family value is to value your husband's family and vice versa. When you have a chance, sit down and list all the good things about your in-laws. With some family members, it will be quite easy to make this list, with others it might be more difficult. If you find it difficult, then I'd recommend the bestselling book *The Blessing* (Pocket Books, 1990). In this book, family counselors Gary Smalley and John Trent, Ph.D., show us how we can transform our lives—even when it is no longer possible to receive our parents' blessing, and they offer practical, effective methods to heal broken hearts and families.

> Whether you have the perfect in-laws or difficult in-law relations, it's important to value family, establish healthy boundaries, and minimize conflict.

Once you've thought of the characteristics, acts, and facts about your extended family for which you can be grateful, make it a point to express your gratitude. For example, if one of the things you value in your mother-in-law is that she gets a lot done, make a point of praising her for this admirable characteristic by saying something like, "Mom, I admire how much you can get done in any given day. I hope I can be as productive as you are one day." You can say this with honesty, even if you know that she is sometimes critical of the fact that you aren't as productive.

When we focus on the things that our in-laws have done right, it builds our estimation of them, and naturally they respond well to this genuine expression of value. It also keeps our focus on the negative at a minimum. We can't control our in-laws but we can choose the kind of attitude we will have toward them. They won't be perfect—that's guaranteed—but we can choose to overlook the negative as much as our personal boundaries will allow.

Establish Healthy Boundaries

I read a book called *Irregular People* by Joyce Landorf Heatherly (Balcony Publishers, 1989) that really changed the way I interact with difficult people that I'm related to by blood or by marriage. Heatherly calls them "irregular people" because they don't always react, interact, or act in a way that is conducive to healthy relationships. My husband, Bob, would just say, "They're weird!" but I wouldn't say that because my editor probably wouldn't let me get away with it! But let's face it, sometimes we all act a little weird, and that's why boundaries are so important.

Lines of Respect

In his bestselling book *Love Must Be Tough* (Word, 1996), Dr. James Dobson introduces the idea of drawing a line of respect with your mate. After I read this book, I found that Dr. Dobson's principles were helpful in my other relationships as well. This line of respect is an essential boundary that you establish over time in your marriage. It is explicitly defined and lovingly held.

We can't control our in-laws but we can choose the kind of attitude we will have toward them.

Draw Your Lines

So if a line of respect is healthy and necessary with our in-laws, then how do we draw it? It works best when your husband draws the line with his parents and you draw it with yours. Basically you establish the boundaries for your marriage and specifically your parents' involvement in those areas. You address the *behavior* but you never attack the *person* in a situation.

Give Me an Example

Cynthia, from our opening story, had a mother who was very controlling and would call at least once a day and sometimes several times a day. Not surprisingly, Chuck began to resent what he felt was an intrusion from his mother-in-law. (Of course, they didn't have a real great start to begin with!) So Cynthia called her mom, and here's the short version of what she said: "Mom, I love you and I appreciate you and your concern for me and my marriage. But I think it's important that I learn to make my own way and make my own decisions as well. The constant phone calls have begun to wear away at my resolve to establish my own marriage's identity, so I think it would be better if we didn't talk every single day. It would be nice to set up a special day during the week that could be just mom/daughter time, and we can discuss anything you'd like at that time."

What About Their Response?

People who like to control usually do not respond well to limitations on their ability to control, and this was the case with Cynthia's mom. It was difficult, but Cynthia had to choose her marriage over her mother, and she made the right choice. Sometimes you just have to take comfort in the fact that you made the right choice, especially when reactions aren't as you hoped they would be.

What If My Husband Won't Do His Part?

"It's hard enough to draw your own lines without having to draw your husband's too," is what my friend Rebecca told me when we were discussing boundaries. She had a mother-in-law who would not accept her daughter-in-law. Every time they were together, she'd belittle her with subtle and not-so-subtle verbal jabs. Rebecca's husband, John, sat idly by, wishing he were out fishing. So after much careful thought and a few tear-filled prayers, Rebecca had to draw her own line. And there were a couple of different ways she could have handled it.

The Less-Than-Ideal Approach

This is the interaction that Rebecca played through in her mind many, many times as she stewed and let resentment build toward her mother-in-law:

> *Mother-in-Law:* Well, you guys are late again; I suppose it took Rebecca an extra hour to put on all that makeup.
>
> *Rebecca:* No, actually, I wasn't the reason we were late today, because we're not late. You're just trying to find something to complain about. And as to my makeup, if you would try a little bit of it every now and then, maybe you wouldn't be a Medusa look-a-like, you old wind bag. Now, why don't you just stop ragging on me or I'll give you a few more choice words that will curl that stringy, lifeless hair of yours!

A Different Approach—Gaining Your Spouse's Support Ahead of Time

Rebecca: (When they were alone, before they went to her in-laws) John, we've talked about your mom's response to me many times, and for whatever reason, you don't seem to want to address the issue with her.

John: Um, do you mind if I organize my fishing tackle box while we talk?

Rebecca: This won't take long. I've just read *Love Must Be Tough,* and I feel that if you will not curb your mom's treatment of me, then I will have to do something myself. I want to get along, and I want to spend time with your parents because they love you and I love you, but I just can't handle being treated that way.

John: (Breathing a sigh of relief) Well, okay. What are you going to say to her, and what am I supposed to do after you say it?

Rebecca: I'm going to establish a line of respect, and if she won't follow it, I want you to agree that you will support me, and we will both leave if necessary.

John agreed, and when they went to his parents' house, here's what happened:

A Different Approach

Mother-in-Law: Well, you guys are late again; I suppose it took Rebecca an extra hour to put on all that makeup.

Rebecca: Actually, we're not late according to my watch, but I hope it's not too late for something else. I want to salvage our relationship because I love your son, but I cannot continue to be treated with disrespect. I know you love your family, and I want to love you, so I'm asking you to please stop making remarks that cut me down and start treating me with respect. John and I have discussed this and agreed that if we can't all speak kindly to each other, then we cannot stay. The choice is yours, but these are the boundaries we feel we must uphold and ask you to respect when we are together.

Mother-in-Law: John, what is this? Are you going to let her sit there and talk to me this way?

John: To be honest, Mom, if I would have thought more about my wife than fishing, I would have said those words myself. I want Rebecca to be treated with respect because

I love her and she's my wife—she deserves it. I love you too, Mom, but I won't sit here and let you treat Rebecca that way anymore.

In this particular case, John finally stepped up to the plate when he saw what a heavy hitter his wife was up against. He did the right thing, and I wish I could tell you that things worked out great and the mother-in-law did a 180 immediately. But it didn't happen that way. However, the good news is that the marriage relationship was given its place of prominence, and eventually Rebecca did develop a much better friendship with her husband's mom.

Minimize Conflict

One of the ways you can minimize conflict is to get a few housekeeping duties taken care of right away. Here are a few to consider:

Gifts For example, who will be responsible for Mother's Day, Father's Day, birthdays, and Christmas gifts? Major conflicts can arise if neither one of you buys a Mother's Day card for one of your moms because you assume the other spouse is taking care of it.

Divide and Conquer A simple way to handle the issue of gifts is for each spouse to buy Mother's and Father's Day and birthday cards and/or gifts for their own family, and then one spouse can be designated to buy the Christmas gifts for everyone.

What Do You Call Them? This may seem like a minor issue, but left unanswered it could be a source of ongoing conflict for years to come. Ask your in-laws what they would like you to call them. This isn't a threatening question NOW, but if left undone, it could be at a later time. There is one woman I heard of who never established what to call her mother-in-law, and twenty years later she still doesn't know, so she never calls her anything. Can you imagine how awkward this would be after all this time? So get this point clarified right away.

Go for the Win/Win Whenever there's a conflict with your in-laws, use the communication ideas shared in chapter 5 and purpose to come to "win/win" or "agree to disagree" resolutions.

Visits A lot of your visiting schedule with family will be determined by how close you live to them. Set some boundaries for these visits so that you can maximize your time with family but still have the individuality to grow and bond as a couple.

Trips If your family doesn't live nearby, use the guide from chapter 13 to help you establish a time when you will take a trip to visit family. Be sure to consider your budget and never go into debt to make a visit happen.

Gifts From Family Carefully consider whether or not to receive financial gifts from in-laws. There could be strings attached or it could lead to conflict in your relationship with your spouse. You want to feel independent from parents, and accepting money keeps you dependent on them. Bob and I made it a policy never to accept large cash sums from my parents apart from a special event or holiday—we didn't want to get into this habit, and the practice has served us well. We have the satisfaction of having earned the things in our home, and while we value the gifts from extended family, there's something special about accumulating things as a couple.

Special Cases

Abuse In this final section, it's important to bring out the point that in the case of a history of abuse in a family, special measures must be taken. If either partner has parents who abused them physically, emotionally, or sexually, it is vitally important to your marriage that you seek professional counseling to work through these issues. Forgiving a parent isn't the same as trusting them again. Forgiveness is freely given, but trust must be earned.

Stepfamilies The dynamics of extended family are multiplied when your parents or your spouse's parents have been divorced and/or remarried. Remember that you will have to make choices based on what you and your spouse determine is best for you as a couple. Your new marriage is the priority—not pleasing everyone, because that just won't happen. Divorce is usually very ugly, and ex-spouses can often become embittered. Sometimes these parents give their adult children an "either/or" ultimatum, which is incredibly selfish on the parents' part. Don't be bullied or manipulated by their bitterness. Try to include all family members as much as possible and make choices for the betterment of your marriage. An excellent resource is *The Smart StepFamily* by Ron Deal (Bethany House, 2002).

Singles If you or your spouse is an only child, it can seem that there is a lot of parental pressure on you. But whether you are the only child or one of eight, the deciding factors on time spent with your parents should be the same—a decision you and your spouse make together. On the other hand, you or your spouse may be a child of a single parent, and this can also add stress to the decision-making process. If you are having trouble being objective in these cases, talk it over with a trusted pastor or family counselor to help you come to a guilt-free decision regarding the extent of your involvement in a single situation.

What Do YOU Call Your In-Laws?

Name	What It Means	Another Option
Hey!	You don't know what to call them.	Ask, "What name do you want me to call you?"
Mr. or Mrs. Brown	Formal and traditional. Possibly detached—or—another culture.	Ask, "Do you want me to call you Mrs. Brown?" (They might want you to call them something less formal.)
Mom or Dad	Close family ties or a desire to have a closer relationship or even a controller.	If your own parents are still living, be sure they know what you'll call your in-laws.
Mother or Father	More formal than Mom, less formal than Mrs. Brown.	This can be a good distinction from your own mom and dad.
Joyce or Tom	Less formal than Mrs. but not quite as intimate as Mom.	Never call your in-laws by their first name unless they have asked you to or you have asked them first.
The Old Man or the Old Lady or the Old Bat or the Old Battle-Ax or worse	It's safe to assume you don't have the greatest relationship with them.	Review this chapter and chapter 5, or get some counseling before you have kids—or they may one day call you the same.
Grandma, Grandpa, Nana, Paw-Paw, Abuela, Abuelo, Noonie and Toonie, or any variety of strange grandparent names	You've given your in-laws one of the best gifts they'll ever get in this lifetime—grandchildren.	Be sure to establish a name for each set of grandparents so your children won't be confused.

CHAPTER 14

WHERE'S THE MONEY, HONEY?

Mapping Out a Sound Financial Future: Steer Clear of Debt and Credit!

Bob and I hopped into the car, ready to embark on a new adventure—a road trip. This time we were going to El Paso for the day, and we were excited about seeing the "Gate to Mexico."

As we pulled out of the driveway, I asked Bob, "Where's the map?"

"Map?" he replied. "Didn't *you* get the map?"

Sigh.

So we went back for the map, bagged it, and headed out again.

"Honey?" I asked, "I didn't notice if you closed the garage door when we left just now, did you?"

"Uh, I thought *you* closed the garage door." He shrugged. "I think it's closed..."

Sigh.

So we went back to make sure the garage door was shut. It was.

At last we were on the open highway, ready to conquer the *tiendas* in the Gate of Mexico and eat some killer tacos at "Si Señor's Casa." *Ah, this is the life!* I thought. And then it hit me—another question. Even though we were an hour down the highway, and I was afraid to ask, I felt I had to. I braced myself for some spousal flak and blurted out:

"Did you bring our cash?"

Bob looked frustrated, but managed to calmly ask *me*, "Did *you* bring it?"

"No, and we can't get more out of the cash machine, because the cash we already withdrew was all we had budgeted for this trip," I reasoned. Then I added, "We'll have to go get the money, honey."

Sigh.

So instead of *tiendas* and tacos, we settled for tuna and the tube—at home!

Sometimes our best-made plans don't always work out to our satisfaction. Either we're forgetful, preoccupied, undisciplined, or just unlucky. When something goes wrong in a marriage—whether it's a car trip or a checkbook—it's easy to try to blame your partner. Money problems continue to be a primary source of conflict in a marriage, and nothing can get you into greater financial stress than debt. One of the single most important things you can do for your future is to stay out of debt.

In his bestselling book *Debt-Free Living*, Larry Burkett says, "It is interesting that the increase in the American divorce rate can be tracked on a curve matching the growth of debt in this country." Debt doesn't benefit a marriage or a family, and it certainly doesn't benefit your future together. You may want to consider the following:

Reasons to Avoid Debt

- Debt makes you a servant to the lender (Proverbs 22:7).
- Debt borrows from your future.
- Debt hinders sharing with others.
- Debt limits your freedom.
- Debt erodes resources through high-interest payments.
- Debt promotes impulse buying.

On the other hand, those who are debt-free have the ability to give generously in order to meet the financial needs of others. There are fewer arguments over money in a household with a low-debt liability. You can answer your phone and not worry about needing an answering machine to screen calls from creditors. The anxiety over floating the bills to make the minimum payments will not exist in a home that follows sound financial principles.

Expanding Debt

Some people allow themselves to sink deeper into debt in anticipation of future pay raises to cover the payments. This has always been a dangerous assumption, but even more so in our volatile economy, when layoffs are becoming commonplace. Many families are simply not aware of how overwhelming a problem debt is until it's almost too late, and they find themselves in bankruptcy court.

Money problems continue to be a primary source of conflict in a marriage and nothing can get you into greater financial stress than debt.

My friend Jaye Ann told me about the time she was in Wal-Mart waiting in line to make a purchase. The woman in front of her was in her early twenties and was holding up the line due to a credit card problem.

"Oh," the young woman said indifferently, "that card is probably maxed out, try this one." She thrust another card into the cashier's hand as she continued, "And if that one doesn't work, we can put part of it on the first and the other part on the second."

The young woman was not disturbed as she remarked nonchalantly to Jaye Ann, "I have almost all my credit cards at their limit. I just pay the minimum balance each month and use it up to the limit again."

She raised her chin, as if to defend herself, "I may be at my credit card limit—but I'm able to get whatever I want."

This young woman knows nothing about delayed gratification. She could be the poster child for a debt-laden society. This destructive mindset has as its motto: "All that matters is getting what you want when you want it." They don't realize that one day this increasing debt will make them pay a price much higher than they should be willing to pay.

Here is a chart that vividly indicates the accumulating debt load for a family who spends only $100 more per month than they earn. We are assuming an average credit card interest of 18 percent compounded monthly for fifteen years.

Year	Amount Overspent	Accumulated Interest	Year-End Balance
1	$1,200	$104	$1,304
2	1,200	463	2,863
3	1,200	1,128	4,728
4	1,200	2,157	6,957
5	1,200	3,621	9,621
6	1,200	5,608	12,808
7	1,200	8,217	16,617
8	1,200	11,572	21,172
9	1,200	15,818	26,618
10	1,200	21,129	33,129
11	1,200	27,714	40,914
12	1,200	35,821	50,221
13	1,200	45,749	61,439
14	1,200	57,855	74,655
15	1,200	72,562	90,562
Totals	$18,000	$72,562	$90,562

This chart vividly illustrates how a modest amount of accumulating debt can cause a family's finances to self-destruct. The family indicated would more than likely have destroyed itself financially well before the fifteen-year point.

Warning Signs

You may not know if you really have a debt problem yet, so here are some indicators that you are heading for a financial fall.

- Using credit card cash advances to pay for living expenses.
- Using and depending on overtime to meet the month's expenses.
- Using credit to buy things that you used to pay cash for (i.e., groceries, gasoline, clothing).
- Using the overdraft protection plan on your checking account to pay monthly bills.
- Using savings to pay bills.
- Using one credit card to pay another.
- "Floating" the bills: delaying one bill in order to pay another overdue bill.
- Using another loan or an extension on a loan to service your debt.
- Using a co-signature on a note.
- Paying only the minimum amount due on charge accounts.

Is there hope for those who already have a sizeable amount of debt? Is it any use even *trying* to manage debt? The answer is a resounding "YES." Getting out of debt may be easier than you think, even major debt, such as a house. Here are some tips to cut down on your debt.

The Power of Prayer

Bob and I have experienced the incredible miracle of answered prayer in the area of seemingly insurmountable debt. When we got married, we had $40,000 in consumer debt. We were like many other young people who didn't realize the price we would pay for instant gratification.

We purposed to get out of debt and made immediate changes in our lifestyle to accomplish this. We also pledged to tithe 10 percent of all we made. We ended up living on less than 25 percent of one income in order to accomplish these goals.

Within two years we were debt-free!

Incredible?

Yes.

Impossible?

No.

Even though the process may be challenging, you will not regret the result. I can't promise you'll reduce your debt as quickly as we did, but once you begin to whittle away at debt, you are on your way to becoming debt-free. You need to start someplace, and praying over your finances is a good place to start.

Couple Meeting

It usually takes more than one partner to get a couple into serious debt. Even if one person does most of the spending, the other spouse usually tolerates the destructive behavior in some way.

Arrange a meeting time to write down goals on paper so that you will have a tangible and objective standard to work toward. The goal you set should include: (1) how to stop spending more than you make; (2) how to pay the interest on the debt you have accumulated; and (3) how to repay the debt.

No More Debt!

If you cannot commit to the standard of no more debt, perhaps it would be wise to seek professional counseling. Financial mismanagement may simply be a symptom of other unresolved issues. The next section lists some helps in this area.

I would recommend that you cut up all but one or two credit cards and cancel all other open credit accounts. This will help minimize the temptation to impulse buy as well as serve to keep you within your goal of no new debt.

The credit card you keep should offer a grace period of at least twenty-five days. It should only be used for convenience and be paid off within twenty-five days or you might need to eliminate that card too.

If you or your spouse lacks the discipline to use this credit card properly, it should be kept in a drawer at home and not carried in your wallet.

Face the Facts

A critical part of assessing your situation is to list all the following information on columnar paper:

Creditor
Balance on each account
Minimum payment
Number of payments left
Interest rate
Item purchased
Due date

Once this information has been documented in one place, it will be easier to ascertain your true debt load and develop a systematic plan to get out of debt.

If you have a serious debt problem (as indicated by the warning signals and the exercise above), you require the help of a professional. The easiest way to find a reputable financial counselor is by looking in your Yellow Pages for Consumer Credit Counseling Services. This is a nonprofit organization designed to help you get out of debt. Or you could call 1–800–4DEBT HELP.

Cut Costs

If your debt load is modest, it can usually be handled by a lifestyle simplification plan designed to help you cut costs and live within or below your means.

The easiest step is to reduce variable expenses, or those monthly expenses that are not fixed like mortgage and car payments. The ideas in *Shop, Save, and Share* as well as my second book, *How to Save Money Every Day,* have helped thousands of families cut costs and get out of debt.

A more dramatic approach would be to reduce your fixed expenses by trading down in a home and/or car in order to get out of debt. This is an issue that you will need to decide based on your desire to become debt-free and the severity of your financial situation.

If you will reduce your standard of living to allow for a monthly debt reduction program, it will be that much easier to become debt-free. You will also need to commit *all* extra income toward debt reduction.

Here are some unexpected sources of income that should be applied toward debt reduction:

inheritance
income tax refund
overtime pay
bonus
insurance dividend refund
pay raise
any other unexpected additional income

Debt Consolidation

If you are going to consolidate your accounts in order to lower the interest rate, purpose to do this only to lower the rates and *not* to extend debt. It's important to be sure that you don't add to your debt by extending it, even if it is offered.

You should only go to this option under the watchful eye of a financial counselor.

Credit Cards

How do you know if you are getting a good value for the credit cards you currently have? You want a card that charges a low-rate (not just a temporary introductory rate) that is fixed (not subject to increase) and with no annual fee.

Don't be deceived by some of the "reward" cards—do the math on those cards. For example, most cards that offer frequent-flier-miles require that you earn 25,000 miles (at one mile per dollar $25,000 spent) in order to buy *one* ticket (which averages $250 to $300). This means you are earning one cent for every dollar you spend. These reward cards also subliminally encourage you to overspend on your credit card.

For a list of credit cards by category (low-rate, no annual fee, etc.) go to *www.bankrate.com* or *www.cardtrak.com*. Other tools that are available to help you get the card that is right for you are *www.getsmart.com* or *www.creditcardgoodies.com*.

Paying Down the Principal

I am the first to admit that I'm not a financial planner. I'm just a mom who wanted to stay home with her children and developed a plan to do so. My plan was based on solid financial principles and some of my great-grandma's commonsense strategies.

You can buy an expensive "pay-down kit" from a financial planner or you can just follow some simple steps and watch your debts diminish. Here are a couple of strategies to paying down the principal rather than merely managing the interest:

Pay the original minimum on each credit entry from our "Face the Facts" section above. If you continue to pay the amount of the *original* minimum payment, you will soon find that the required minimum is reduced. If your payment remains at the higher amount, then you are paying on the principal and saving on interest by paying the debt off early.

Pay the most/least first Organize your debts with the highest interest rate and shortest payoff time as the first priority on the list. Once this debt is paid, then apply the total amount of that payment (that you no longer have) to the next bill on your list. Once you get a couple of these "easy payoff" debts off your monthly budget, you will be encouraged by the fact that the *number* of your debts has been reduced. Apply the additional funds to the debt that has the highest interest rate.

Pay your mortgage principal If you pay your monthly mortgage *plus* the principal on the next month's payment, and continue to do this, you will find that your mortgage can be paid off in about half the time. Look at your original mortgage loan and see how little of your initial payments goes toward the principal. You are mainly servicing the interest.

On the other hand, if you make the monthly payment and pay the principal for the next month, and do this every month, it will only increase your payments by a margin (depending on your mortgage payment). All of those additional dollars go directly to the principal. This allows you to pay down the principal rapidly, and with proper planning you could end up paying off a 30-year mortgage in only 15 years!

With proper planning, you could end up paying off a 30-year mortgage in only 15 years!

If you want precise amounts and the exact timing on how to pay your mortgage in half the time, you can invest in a financial calculator (available at electronics stores), or you could contact a volunteer financial counselor. You can find these at online sites such as *www.interest.com/hugh/calc/mort.html.*

Buy Down Your Rate

If you get an unexpected bonus or source of other income, it makes sense to buy down the rate of your mortgage loan.

You can do this by paying points (one point is equivalent to 1 percent of the loan amount). This means that on a $100,000 30-year fixed-rate mortgage at 8.5 percent, you could lower the rate to 8 percent by paying $2,000 up front. As long as you stay in the house for five years, you'll recoup the money.

This tip works well when rates are not projected to come down over the next few years. If there is a prediction of falling rates, it would be wiser to use your buy-down money during a refinance to get a lower-than-low rate.

Rebuilding Good Credit

A bankruptcy will stay on your credit report at least eight years. Even after you've rebuilt credit after this severe kind of damage, you won't be able to qualify for rock-bottom mortgage rates. According to Jean Sherman Chatzky, financial editor at *USA Weekend Magazine* (Jan. 21, 2000), these are the things that will have to be done to rebuild your credit rating:

Close accounts you don't use. To lenders, charge accounts or home-equity lines of credit mean you could go on a spending spree at any time.

Don't hit all your credit limits. If you're using 80 percent or more of your available credit, it's a sign to lenders that you're overextended.

Limit inquiries into your credit record. Minimize the number of times you apply for credit, because each inquiry will appear on your credit report, whether you get the credit or not. Keep in mind that all inquiries for one purpose, such as a mortgage, will count as one.

Don't miss payments. Automate as many payments as possible, if you can keep up with these automated payments in your accounts at home. If you make sure the funds are there, you will never be late on payments. Everyone from health clubs to electric companies have these services available.

Check your credit report. Order a copy from any of the major credit bureaus: Equifax (800-685-1111), Experian (888-297-3742), or Trans Union (800-888-4213). This report costs about eight dollars. If you live in Colorado, Georgia, Maryland, Massachusetts, New Jersey, or Vermont, or if you've been denied credit before, you qualify for a free copy annually. It makes sense to take advantage of this service.

CHAPTER 15

THE THINGS THAT MATTER MOST

How to Simplify Your Life and Focus on the Things That Last

McDonald's is a hallowed spot for this little old gal from Texas. I have good memories from that American institution while growing up. When my mom and I went shopping, we usually took Abuela, my Spanish grandmother. This generous, hardworking woman often treated us to lunch at McDonald's from the money she earned laboring in the kitchen clean-up area of a retirement home. I remember standing in line waiting for my 23¢ hamburger and singing the Big Mac song: "Two whole beef patties, special sauce, lettuce, cheese, pickles, onions on a sesame seed bun." If I was really good, Abuela would buy me a 15¢ Coke. That was before the days of free refills, so I had to make it last. If it was Christmas or my birthday, then I might get half of a hot apple pie for 21¢. Those were the days—simple pleasures for a simple life.

Several years ago, when Joshua was a baby, and the other kids were ages two, four, five, and seven, I took my kids to "Mickey D's." As I waited in line, I recalled the simple days of my childhood and my Spanish grandmother. My musing abruptly came to an end when the server asked, "Welcome to McDonald's. May I take your order, please?"

I had a sense of dejá vu as I set Joshua down on the counter and fought an urge to imitate my grandmother and ask, "Do chew have any tacos?"

Instead, I placed my order. "Yes, I'll take five Happy Meals, please."

The young cashier looked at Joshua, who had grabbed her pen and was teething on it. She looked at me as if I'd just spoken in another language, and asked, "What did you say?"

Did I accidentally speak in my Spanish or something? I wondered to myself.

I removed the pen from the baby's mouth and returned it, somewhat wet, to the cash register and repeated my order: "I'll take five Happy Meals, *please.*"

The befuddled girl looked up and didn't see any of my other children around—they were in the playground. So she repeated herself. "Did you say *five* Happy Meals?"

Frustration was starting to kick in by now, especially with Joshua's attempt to crawl into the ketchup stash under the counter. I really wanted to get this order placed. After all, I'd waited in line a long time. Sighing deeply and looking the girl squarely in the eye, I repeated myself a third time. "Yes, I said *five* Happy Meals—*to eat here, now*—please."

The dutiful employee's look of amazement turned into suspicion. I was afraid she was about to call the Happy Meal Police.

Is there a limit as to how many Happy Meals an individual can order? I asked myself.

The cashier *finally* placed my order and I paid for the meals. Somewhat impatiently, I waited for my order to be processed.

I put Joshua back on my hip and stood back from the counter while the McTeam assembled hamburgers, French fries, and mini Mr. Potato Head toys.

Great, what are we going to do with five potato heads? I thought as I pictured hundreds of tiny moustaches and ears strewn about the house.

Joshua stuck his hand in my mouth as an employee brought the tray of five Happy Meals. As I walked away, balancing a tray of food and a busy baby boy, I heard the employee whisper to her counterpart:

And I thought I was the only adult who liked Happy Meals!

There are plenty of days when I wish I could just take a day off from life, sit under the golden arches, and eat a Happy Meal. Life is so complicated and just plain busy. Children today are involved in more extracurricular activities than any previous generation. The "simple life" is just an old song at the opening of the movie *Father of the Bride*. Some of our lives are so complicated that figuring out an income tax return makes for a relaxing evening at home.

We have tons of options and opportunities that are often obstacles to the simple life. At the end of the day, we're often exhausted from the full life filled with busyness. At one time or another everyone feels, as the Air Force says, "over-tasked and undermanned."

> Now is a good time to keep a handle on simplyfying your life.

Since you and your husband are just starting your new life together, *now* is a good time to keep a handle on simplifying your life. There's sometimes a misconception among those who are newly married that life will slow down and become simpler when your family starts to expand. Well, that's simply not true. There's no day like today to learn how to live the simple life. If the research put into this chapter helps you as much as it helped me, you won't feel as if you're still a few fries short of a Happy Meal.

Ideas to Simplify Your Life

Tips From a Bunny

Ever since she was old enough to hold a crayon, our daughter Bethany, also known as "Bunny," has been a writer. She comprised some 5,247 works of prose in her first decade on this planet. They're posted on our refrigerator, Bob's desk at work, my computer monitor, and the toilet seat cover. We've got our Bunny's "cottage industry products" on the rearview mirror in the car, the bathroom mirror, and my compact powder mirror. They are a reflection of her soul.

Yes, I suppose I'm biased, but I think this little girl has talent. She writes, colors, and pastes her way into the hearts of friends and family, neighbors, and even acquaintances. Bethany has the uncanny ability to see the best in others. She encourages people when the world beats them down and leaves them for lost.

Take, for instance, the time we met a VERY large woman while we were waiting in a doctor's office. This lady, clinically labeled as "morbidly obese," was at least one hundred pounds overweight. At the time, Bethany was three and Philip was five (the age of brutal honesty). I imagined this woman lived a life filled with rejection and judgment—it couldn't have been easy for her. I was concerned about Philip's honesty, so I sent him to get a drink of water down the hallway—a standing gag order. That left Bethany and me alone with the woman.

While my "kindness" was to politely ignore the woman, pretending she wasn't there, Bethany talked to her. She soon discovered the lady's name was June. She told June about her doll, bunny collection, and Papa's airplane. Then Bethany looked into June's puffy face and sweetly said, "You have beautiful hair."

June's face brightened as she returned Bethany's smile. "Thank you, Bethany, my father always used to tell me that too." There were tears glistening in her eyes as she said, "He's been gone for fifteen years now."

Bethany's observation was true. June's only beautiful *physical* trait was her honey-blond hair. My little girl can see the beauty where others see the unlovely. How long had it been since anyone paid this woman a compliment? Who knows, it could have been fifteen years.

Bethany has been given the unique gift that can turn an uncomfortable situation into the divine. She shares a spontaneous love of the Father with those who are hurting in her tiny world. She lets people know, in a little girl way, that they are beloved of the Father. She takes complex rejection and creates simple acceptance.

You too can bring joy and love into the lives of others by showing acceptance to your husband, your co-workers, the clerks or cashiers who assist you. The next time you're in a waiting room, or in a line, or taking a coffee break, look beyond the surface of the people standing next to you and see if you've got a smile or word of encouragement that they desperately need. The amazing part of this simple act of kindness is that it can make you as hopping happy as our bunny, Bethany.

Assess the "A" List

We can learn something from a happy bunny. Take our schedules, for instance. If we think about the beautiful in the midst of an ugly, busy schedule—we too can bring simplicity out of complexity. We might follow Bethany's example through writing. Why not write a list of *everything* on your schedule for the past two weeks? List the regular commitments and responsibilities, the daily tasks, and additional duties. Don't forget the activities of your spouse; they impact your life too. As a final note, add up the hours spent in front of the television and on the computer.

You should have a substantial list compiled at the end of this homework assignment. I sure did—I didn't realize I was doing so much *stuff* until it was written down. When we look at our lives in black and white we have to ask the age-old question: "Why?"

Why am I spending so much time pursuing activities that are unimportant and not urgent? Aren't these time-wasters in the scheme of life? Why does busywork, phone calls, and trivia take the place of planning, recreation, and relationship building?

In *Seven Habits of Highly Effective People*, Stephen Covey says, "To say 'yes' to important . . . priorities, you have to learn to say 'no' to other activities, sometimes apparently urgent things" (156). When we write these activities down on paper, we can prioritize and evaluate the importance of the "stuff" that fills our schedules—and our lives.

I have a daily prayer that has helped me simplify life that you may want to consider as a couple:

Father, please help me to do the things that are truly important today, and to be content to let fall by the wayside those things that don't really matter.

Now evaluate your "A list," or activities list. What activities are unimportant and yet still on your list? Do you have time for the *important*, or only the *urgent?* You could even pray about your schedule and ask God to help take the complex and make it a little simpler.

Bangles, Baubles, and Beads

As a teenager, I used to spend hours playing the "Catalog Game." I'd take a Best Products catalog and turn to the jewelry section. At each page, with the product prices covered, I would ask myself the same question: "If you could have any piece of jewelry on this page, which would you pick?" I'd hem and haw (a regular pastime for a Texan), and then I'd pick my "favorite." I'd check the price, and if it was the most expensive piece on the page—I won! It proved I had good taste.

This pastime was a private pleasure—or so I thought. But one day my dad caught me poring over the catalog and laughed. "Oh, Ellie, you're one for bangles, baubles, and beads." Not understanding what he meant at the time, it sounded like a put-down. But I know what he means now. The triple B accessories can take over your life if you let them.

Guys don't have this problem. They put on a uniform, a suit and tie, or a T-shirt and jeans, and they're set to go. Women, on the other hand, have to scrounge through their *bangles* to find their *baubles* and then locate a matching *bead*. We can simplify life by avoiding the temptation to become obsessed with things. If we pore over new-car brochures, we're less likely to be content with the car we have now. If we window-shop at the mall too often, we're likely to overspend there.

There's an old saying: "I can look in the window if I don't buy anything." Well, if you don't even make a habit of looking in the window, you'll be less likely to buy things that don't compliment your finances and, ultimately, your marriage.

Quality Simplifies

At my house, the "triple B" problem was taken care of about ten years ago when I decided to have one set of jewelry to wear every day. They are quality pieces, made of real gold and gems. I have a wedding ring, anniversary band (a decoration for service *above and beyond the call of duty*), a simple gold necklace and matching bracelet, a pair of 18K antique gold earrings (Bob brought back for me from Desert Storm), and my Seiko watch.

My watch was a wonderful find. My "motherlike" friend, Madeline, found it in the mud in her cow pasture fifteen years ago when she was doing the "pioneer thing." Who knows how long it had been in the field. The family had owned the property for about five years when she found it.

At any rate, it was still ticking. In the past fifteen years, I've replaced the crystal once and the battery a few times. The watch has served me well because quality lasts. Besides that, it looks good, and it simplifies.

I don't have to hunt through piles of fake jewelry to find two earrings that match—I save time. I'm not constantly losing bracelets or shopping for the latest fad—I save money. I'm not at the mercy of the materialistic, mundane, or maniacal—I've saved frustration.

Besides my everyday jewelry, I have a few pieces of quality "dress-up" jewelry, including a crown pin my friend Brenda gave me for my birthday. She says it's supposed to remind me that I'm a coupon queen. The fancy stuff is worn to church on Sunday, formal functions, speaking engagements, and Daniel's basketball awards ceremony—they're saved for the really important events. These pieces are quality, and they help simplify my life.

Get Rid of the Junk

There's a basic philosophy at the Kay house about the stuff we accumulate over the years: *Junk has the ability to accumulate according to the amount of storage space available.* Several years ago we moved to a house with extra storage. We thought, *Oh, great—more space.* At first we had some extra breathing room. In a matter of a few months we filled the space with junk. We found ourselves, once again, overpowered by the self-imposed pressure of STUFF!

Now I go through all the boxes *before* they make it into a storage room. We chuck the junk and store more. Every six months we sort through all five of the children's clothing, toys, and junk—getting rid of the ties that bind and gag. Sure it takes a full day's effort to purge ourselves of the perplexing pile. But the result is worth it—a refreshed soul.

As a newlywed you may already have an accumulation of junk from two combined households, and you could stand to go through it all. But if you don't have that much right now, try to keep it that way and make it a habit to regularly streamline your stuff.

It's the Little Things That Count

When we moved from New Mexico to upstate New York, we wanted to be inconspicuous travelers. However, we had to take enough clothing for four months (for seven people), food for the 3,000-mile trip (we just had to dip through Texas—ya'll hear?), and equipment for the camper we were pulling. If you can picture it, we had a cherry red Suburban (with a massive travel pod on top) pulling a 21-foot travel trailer (including five bicycles strapped on an exterior bike rack). There were kids hanging out the windows, and Barney underwear flying in the wind (who stuck that in the trailer door?). We were inconspicuous, all right.

When people passed us on the highway, they were either laughing or shaking their heads—even after we pulled the undies back into the trailer. I felt a lot like "Granny" on the Beverly Hillbillies. All we needed was my rocker strapped on top of the luggage rack—but that's where Bob drew the line.

When we added up all the "little things" we needed for our trip and temporary living, we found we were hauling 5,000 pounds—the bare minimum. Bob is a master packer. His motto: "Stuff and cram."

It's amazing how all the little things in our lives add up, clogging up the sleek machinery and draining us of our energy. Simplifying, even in little things, can help loads. It's the little things like habits, hobbies, and the accumulation of stuff that tend to complicate our lives. I'll close out this chapter with a list of "little things." If you start thinking about your idea of simplicity, you'll come up with a lot more. In the process, I think you'll also find a lot more breathing room.

Drink Water

This little tip helps our waistlines, wallets, and well-being (no pun intended). We all know we should drink more water, but it has to become a habit—it doesn't come naturally. I've heard that if you do anything consistently for twenty-one days, it becomes a habit. At first you have to remind yourself to practice the positive action. Day four or five seems to be the hardest. But once you've done it regularly for at least twenty-one days, it becomes automatic.

Drinking water, as a habit, refreshes our physical bodies and makes us healthier. Drinking water saves all kinds of money spent at the grocery store on other beverages. Drinking water saves the hassle of recycling cans, plastic, and bottles. Drinking water is a small, refreshing way to simplify. I found that a good way to get into the habit is to keep a filled water bottle in my car, at my desk, or along with me on my workout.

Turn Out the Intruder

Were you completely honest when you made a written list of your weekly activities? You *did* make a list, didn't you? If you are like most folks, you had anywhere from thirty to forty hours of television (or videos, computer games, or "surfing the net" time) on your schedule. Try keeping a media log of each family member's time on the PC, VCR, DVD, or TV—for just a few days. You'll be amazed.

> We limit TV time, and this simplifies. We don't have to rush around, catching up on responsibilities, because we've wasted countless hours in front of the tube.

One of the reasons Bob and I get so much done each day is that we've turned out the intruder. For the first five years of our marriage, we refused to get a TV set. My father and brother brought their own TV to our house on Thanksgiving so they could have their football fix. We got a video monitor in our sixth year of marriage and have a television now—but no cable.

It's so easy to let this intruder eat up family relationships and productivity time. I'll watch an occasional video while clipping coupons, or we'll watch a family video on special evenings. We limit TV time, and this simplifies. We don't have to rush around, catching up on responsibilities, because we've wasted countless hours in front of the silly tube.

Let's face it, apart from some family-oriented network trends, most of the stuff on television is the same kind of stuff that fills our storage space—junk. Throw it out and get a life—the simple life.

Easy Care

Instead of buying clothing that has to be dry-cleaned, pressed, and starched—try buying easy-care clothing instead. Sometimes you don't have a choice, but often you can just as easily choose a wash-and-wear article of clothing as a dry-clean-only item. The time you spend running to the dry cleaners and the $10 to $15 you save on your weekly laundry bill is well worth the choice.

Quit Your Job

Have you ever had a job you despised? Have you ever prayed for a plague to overtake you (or your employer) so you didn't have to go in to work? Is your job so complicated it makes the National Defense Plan look like a game of Tinker Toys? Have you ever quit your job because you loathed your boss? And then at your next job you find your new supervisor is your former boss's evil twin brother, Skippy? Been there. Done that.

Shouldn't we be involved in jobs that utilize our God-given skills, talents, and gifts? Chuck Swindoll, in his radio program *Insight for Living*, said that when people operate within their (spiritual) gifts, it is done "with ease and effectiveness." Think about it. Is your present job done with ease and effectiveness?

In high school my best friend, Donna, and I got jobs as pollsters. We had to call registered voters and ask them who they were voting for—it's also known as a "cold call." Usually I caught the person off guard; it was perceived as a nuisance call, and they hung up the phone— you could say they had a *cold* response. Even though I tried to warm them up, they usually didn't give me the chance. I've never handled rejection well. I hated that job, but it paid eight dollars an hour—a decent wage for a teenager back in the early '80s. Those calls were not made with *ease and effectiveness*. That job didn't simplify my life. Working at a job you hate complicates your life tremendously.

On the other hand, while working as a sales representative in the camera department at Best Products (in high school and college), I excelled. My job seemed simple, because it was enjoyable. People came to me—it wasn't a cold call. Product knowledge came easily—I could tell any customer the difference between a Canon AE–1, an Olympus OM–10, and a Minolta XG–5. A comparison of the various features was delivered with a flash and a smile. As a matter of fact, I was offered the position of assistant manager at the age of eighteen—the youngest manager in the firm. It was a good decision to turn it down, because I didn't want to give up my college classes—it would have complicated my life too much. But it was a flattering offer. You could probably say I operated with ease and effectiveness.

If I had to go back to that job now, the functional part could be done well, but that *kind of job* wouldn't fit in with my current priorities. Also, my skill and education level wouldn't find fulfillment in that position. It was a good position for that particular time in my life, but it wouldn't fit my life now, and working a job that doesn't fit your life *complicates.*

For a number of years my seminar engagements operated in a feast-or-famine cycle—my self-esteem followed the same pattern. When there were many speaking engagements, I felt valued; when there were few, I felt as if I was "nothing more than" a wife and mother. Then God completely shut the door on speaking. For two years the load dropped from five presentations a *month* to only one a *year.* During that season I learned that being a wife and mother *was everything,* and the seminar stuff was secondary. Also, I learned to do my *primary* job, that of mothering, with ease and effectiveness. Then, and only then, did God restore the speaking opportunity. As a matter of fact, the seminars had a greater purpose, power, and response than ever before. That famine season revealed a simple truth: God is the giver of all good gifts.

If you're not operating within your area of ease and effectiveness, look around. You may be operating outside your skill level. You may not be suited to your present job. You may have reached the place where you're no longer challenged. Or, as in my case, you may simply need to learn one of life's lessons in your present job. On the other hand, it may be time for a change—either internally or externally—with your present job. Sometimes the boldest choices involve the greatest risk.

When you're in the wrong job, it adds stress to your life, which can cause normal irritants to escalate. When Bob worked for difficult bosses, he sometimes brought his work home with him, which made tempers flare on the home front. These dynamics are examples of how being in the wrong job complicates your life. But now Bob is flying the F–117, and his motto is "It's great to love going to work in the morning and then love coming back home in the evening—life doesn't get any better than that!"

CHAPTER 16

ONE DOWN, FORTY-NINE TO GO!

When Bob and I celebrated our first anniversary, we lived in base housing that featured ancient tile floors from the '60s and cinder block walls that required a drill in order to hang pictures. Because we had so much debt, our home was decorated in a vintage secondhand store motif. But it was home to us, and we will always remember that first year fondly.

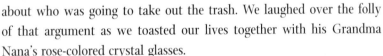

Making the First Anniversary Celebration Special

Our first anniversary dinner was served on my Great-Grandma Laudeman's antique Spode china and eaten with my Grandma Eleanor's silver. I made Bob's favorite—corned beef and cabbage. The beef was too chewy and the cabbage wasn't cooked thoroughly, but Bob pretended that it was a meal fit for a king. Our "dining room" was in a tiny corner of the old-fashioned kitchen, and we could hear the couple next door arguing about who was going to take out the trash. We laughed over the folly of that argument as we toasted our lives together with his Grandma Nana's rose-colored crystal glasses.

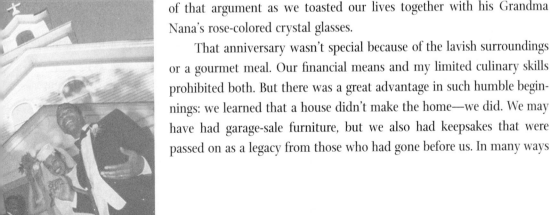

That anniversary wasn't special because of the lavish surroundings or a gourmet meal. Our financial means and my limited culinary skills prohibited both. But there was a great advantage in such humble beginnings: we learned that a house didn't make the home—we did. We may have had garage-sale furniture, but we also had keepsakes that were passed on as a legacy from those who had gone before us. In many ways our grandmas celebrated our joy with us through their china, silver, and crystal on the table. We've come a long way since those humble beginnings, but we will never forget the joy of forging a new life with the one we love.

As I look back on our years together, I'm the most thankful for the fact that we fully enjoyed each other that first year and that we learned how to treat each other with dignity and respect from the beginning. We developed some very good habits, ones that serve us well today as we juggle the responsibility of lots of children and demanding careers.

One day you may be surrounded by other responsibilities, such as children, or a challenging job that takes precedence over spending time with your spouse. The advantage time and experience has given me is that I know time with my husband is the most precious commodity on earth. We have no guarantees in this life: I could be in a car accident or Bob's jet could go down tomorrow. Living with a high-risk professional pilot has taught me not to take life for granted.

Now is a good time to commemorate your wedd• date and make a habit o celebrating it in a significant way.

This first year together is a special one, and it's important that you develop healthy relationship habits early so that you can weather the storms of life—sickness, periods of separation, and the day-to-day crises. While every day can be special, some days are more special than others, and anniversaries are the "most specialest" as our youngest son, Joshua, says. Now is a good time to commemorate your wedding date and make a habit of celebrating it in a significant way.

I know one family, the Grapes, who go away every anniversary, even if it's just for one night. When times were lean financially, they set aside money for this purpose and saved year-round. By using the tips in chapter 3 of this book, you can get the best value for your dollar out of an anniversary trip. But even a trip to a secluded beach in Hawaii won't satisfy you if your relationship isn't hitting on all cylinders. So while you don't want to make a "trip" the focal point of this anniversary, you do want to make it special in all the ways you can. This chapter will give you a variety of ways to help you toward that end.

State of the Union Address

Just as our president will give a State of the Union address, the first anniversary is a perfect time to readdress those issues that you probably covered in premarital counseling. Pick several areas of your marriage and discuss what the current status is in relationship to these topics. This isn't a time to criticize or complain; rather, it is a time to assess and refocus, if necessary.

Here are a few topics to address with regard to your union:

- What is the status of your communication and conflict resolution?
- Are you doing romantic things together that can lead to intimacy?
- How is your intimacy?
- How well do you and your spouse understand the male/female differences that make each of you unique?
- Are your finances in a desirable state?
- Where are you in your spiritual lives together?
- What traditions have you developed this year?
- How are things going with your in-laws?
- What are your schedules like, and do you need to simplify?
- Are you satisfied with the delegation of household chores?
- What do you enjoy about your home, and what plans do you have for it in the future?
- What are the favorite foods your spouse makes, and what do you prepare that he enjoys?
- What activities or hobbies are you enjoying together, and what are some things you'd still like to do or places you would like to go?

Will You Remember Me?

There's a song by Sarah McLachlan called "I Will Remember You" that is a wistful song about remembering true love. Ten, twenty, thirty years from now, you will likely forget many of the details that are fresh in your memory right now—the particulars about your lives together, and especially this first year. Since the first anniversary traditionally calls for "paper" as the gift of choice, why not set up an anniversary memory book? You could fill in the following topics and update it annually with photos and other mementos. It will be interesting and fun to see the way you and your spouse grow as a couple and how your tastes and perspectives change. Here are a few things you might want to include:

Home   Write down your address, take photos of your home, indicate the style in which it is decorated, and list your favorite room or rooms, and why.

Songs   What are your favorites? Why not record a CD of all your faves for your spouse to remember you by when he is driving or is at work. List these songs in your memory book, and be sure to include why they are special to you.

Food   List your favorite restaurant and what makes it so special to you as a couple. What are some of the romantic things you did or said over dinner? What is your hubby's favorite food and what is your best dessert?

Dates   What are some of your most memorable dates this year? It could be the day you first entertained company, or when you heard you were moving, or when you first told your spouse you were sorry for something you said. Mark them and remember them or you will forget over time.

Photos   Pepper your memory book with plenty of photos, and be sure to write where, when, and why they were taken.

Spiritual Mile Markers   What were the highlights in your spiritual life together? What church did you attend? What is the greatest spiritual lesson you learned during this past year?

Friends   Who are your friends and how did you meet them? What are some of the best times you've had together and places you've gone with them?

Fun   What are the funniest events you can think of this past year? For my first year, it was learning how to boil an egg and making a crazy set of curtains for Bob's grandma. Even if something wasn't funny your first month of marriage, you might be able to see the humor in it eleven months from now.

Family What family did you entertain in your home this year? What do you call your mother-in-law? What trips did you make, and how did you celebrate holidays in your family? What are your dreams for your own family, and how many children do you eventually want to have?

> You don't have to spend a lot of money to make your first anniversary special.

Cheap Dates

You don't have to spend a lot of money to make your first anniversary special, even if your schedules or finances prohibit you from taking a trip. Be creative and make it fun. Review the ideas for day trips and other types of inexpensive entertainment in chapter 3. Here are a few more fun ideas to help you plan a memorable anniversary:

Themed Evening A fun way to combine romance and economy is to set up a theme dinner for you and your husband. If you decide to do Chinese food, serve it on a low coffee table and don't wear your shoes—try to find a Kimono-type robe that you can s-l-o-w-l-y remove later. Or serve Italian on a red-and-white-checked cloth with a candle in a bottle and Italian music playing in the background. If you want the feeling of the great outdoors, serve a fried chicken dinner on a tablecloth placed on the floor with fresh flowers in vases around you. Wear a little something special under your shorts and halter-top, and pretend you're lying in a field of flowers for dessert. Try to set up your love play later by carrying the theme from dinner into the bedroom.

Ice Cream Buy a half-gallon of your spouse's favorite ice cream. Take it to a park, throw down a blanket, and eat the entire thing—together, of course!

Golf Anyone? Go to a driving range together and hit a few balls. Make a "bet" on the balls by giving a back rub or other bonus for any drive hit over one hundred yards. Or go to a miniature golf course and kiss him or give him a huge hug for every hole in one!

Culture Broaden your horizons by visiting a local art gallery or museum. Try to analyze what the artist is trying to say and how the piece speaks to you personally. Ask your spouse why he likes or dislikes the work and learn more about him in the process.

Scuba You? You might not be able to afford scuba diving or deep-sea dives, but if you live near a lake, you can go snorkeling. Be sure to kiss your love under the water.

Bowling for Backs Bowling is a very inexpensive form of entertainment. Make it even more interesting by giving a back rub for every game your spouse wins. Or you can have him do a week's worth of laundry if *you* win.

Concert While many concerts are quite pricey, some are free or available at discounts. Check your local paper for tickets that are being sold or the lineup for a free concert series. Take your favorite bottle of wine, some cheese, and a blanket, and hold your love while you listen to others make beautiful music.

Lover Boy You can create a date for your husband and not even be there! When Bob has to travel, I always include a note tucked into his flight bag. Sneak a note into your husband's car, Day-Timer, or mail him one at work.

Double Feature Rent your favorite movies of all time. Have a double feature together with snacks and sodas.

Window Shopping After a dinner or dessert date, go window shopping and ask your spouse to choose all the things he likes that are under twenty dollars, then go back and buy him one of those for no particular reason.

Make Time for Romance

If you'll remember from chapter 5, when a guy says, "Would you like to go to dinner?" he often means, "And I hope it will eventually lead to sex!" Once you've done all the special things you can to make it memorable, keep in mind the intimate part of your day together as you engage in a special time of love play. Here are ten suggestions to enhance your intimacy compiled from my own ideas, Ed Wheat's book *Love Life for Every Married Couple*, and Robert and Debra Bruce's book *Reclaiming Intimacy* (Bethany House, 1996):

Show and Tell Show each other the places on your body you like to be touched that give you special satisfaction. A light touch is often the most thrilling. Use your imagination in the way you caress.

Hold Through the Night Demonstrate to each other how you would like to be held. Kiss your lover the way you like to be kissed, showing them something that they may not have sensed before.

Back Rubs These don't have to be full-blown massages. They can be gentle caresses on the small of the back, up the backbone, and to the back of the neck, right under the hairline.

Slow Down You don't have to rush through this time together. If something feels particularly pleasurable to you or your mate, then take time to enjoy it.

Give and Take Love play isn't only about pleasing the other, it's also about letting the other please you. Take turns in your expressions of love.

Point of Contact As you go to sleep, have your leg touch his, your hand on his shoulder, or your chest against his back. This is a cozy habit Bob and I have, and I will often count how many places our bodies are touching.

Beginning Your Day Even if one partner has to get up early, make a habit of snuggling at the beginning of the day. Let your spouse know how good he feels in your arms and how you wish he didn't have to go to work this morning. Savor the physical contact, even if it's only for a few minutes.

Snuggle It's important, even if you do not end up making love, to spend time every night snuggling in bed. Whisper words of love during this time before you drift off to sleep.

Holding Hands This is beginning to be a lost art, but try to hold hands with your spouse often. Our bodies naturally hunger for physical touch, and holding hands meets this need.

Passing By Dr. Kevin Leman says that women don't like being manhandled, and he's never yet met a woman who says she enjoys being grabbed. If your spouse is in this habit, and you don't enjoy it, then express a different way he can touch you throughout the day. Instead of grabbing you, he could lightly run his fingers down your arm. Let your spouse know the kind of casual touch you enjoy.

Wedding Anniversary Gifts

1st paper or clocks

2nd cotton or china

3rd leather or glass

4th flowers or small appliances

5th wood or silverware

6th iron or candy

7th wool or copper

8th bronze or linen

9th pottery or leather

10th aluminum or diamond

11th steel or jewelry

12th silk or pearls

13th lace or textiles

14th ivory or gold jewelry

15th crystal or watches

20th china or platinum

25th silver

30th pearl

35th coral or jade

40th ruby

45th sapphire

50th gold

55th emerald

60th diamond

One Down, Forty-Nine to Go!

Well, you've made it through the first year, and should God allow, there will be many more years in your future together. But we have no guarantees in life, and it is critically important that we make the most of our days with the ones we love. This book has given some basic and practical ways for you to make the most of your marriage, but reading books has very little value if you don't practice what you learn.

Marriage is probably the toughest job you'll ever love—it is hard work. But no other relationship in life pays the kind of dividends that come from a life of devotion to your mate. May each of your years together grow more and more valuable as your mutual investments expand to the treasures that time brings—memories, children, grandchildren, successfully weathering hardship, deepening love, and a powerful faith in the One that brought you together.

May you find in your spouse a "happily ever after."

> We have no guarantees in life, and it is critically important that we make the most of our days with the ones we love.

General

Chapman, Gary. *The Five Love Languages*. Northfield Publishers, 1992.

Chapman, Steve, and Annie Chapman. *Married Lovers, Married Friends*. Bethany House Publishers, 1989.

Harley, Willard. *His Needs, Her Needs*. Fleming H. Revell, 1997.

Janssen, Al. *Marriage Masterpiece*. Tyndale, 2001.

Kay, Ellie. *Shop, Save, and Share*. Bethany House Publishers, 1998.

———. *How to Save Money Every Day*. Bethany House Publishers, 2001.

Mason, Mike. *Mystery of Marriage*. Multnomah Publishers, new edition 2001.

Parrott, Les, and Leslie Parrott. *Questions Couples Ask*. Zondervan Publishing House, 1996.

———. *Becoming Soul Mates*. Zondervan Publishing House, 1997.

Peace, Martha. *The Excellent Wife*. Focus Publishing, 1997.

Scott, Dr. Stuart. *The Exemplary Husband*. Focus Publishing, 2001.

Smalley, Gary. *If Only He Knew*. Zondervan Publishing House, 1982.

———. *For Better and for Best*. Zondervan Publishing House, 1982.

Smalley, Gary, and John Trent. *Love Is a Decision*. Pocket Books, 1993.

Walker, Jim. *Husbands Who Won't Lead and Wives Who Won't Follow*. Bethany House Publishers, 1989.

Wheat, Ed. *First Years of Forever*. Zondervan Publishers, 1988.

———. *Love Life for Every Married Couple*. Zondervan Publishers, 1980.

Wright, H. Norman. *Communication: Key to Your Marriage*. Regal Books, updated edition 2000.

———. *After You Say I Do*. Harvest House Publishers, 1999.

———. *The Complete Book of Christian Wedding Vows*. Bethany House Publishers, 2001.

Devotional

Arp, David, and Claudia Arp. *Marriage Moments: Heart to Heart Times to Deepen Your Love.* Servant Publications, 1999.

Dobson, Jim, and Shirley Dobson. *Night Light: A Devotional for Couples.* Multnomah, 2000.

Wright, H. Norman. *Quiet Times for Couples.* Harvest House Publishers, 1997.

———. *Together for Good.* Harvest House Publishers, 2000.

Humor

Farrell, Pam, and Bill Farrell. *Men Are Like Waffles, Women Are Like Spaghetti.* Harvest House Publishers, 2001.

Linamen, Karen. *Sometimes I Wake Up Grumpy, Sometimes I Let Him Sleep.* Fleming Revell, 2001.

Meurer, Dave. *Daze of Our Wives.* Bethany House Publishers, 2000.

Prayer

Omartian, Stormie, and Michael Omartian. *The Power of a Praying Wife.* Harvest House Publishers, 1997.

———. *The Power of a Praying Husband.* Harvest House Publishers, 2001.

Sex

Crenshaw, Theresa, M.D. *The Alchemy of Love and Lust: How Our Sex Hormones Influence Our Relationships.* Pocket Books, 1996.

Farrell, Bill, Pam Farrell, Jim Conway, and Sally Conway. *Pure Pleasure.* InterVarsity Press, 1984.

LaHaye, Tim, and Beverly LaHaye. *The Act of Marriage.* Zondervan Publishers, 1998.

Lepine, Bob, and Dennis Rainey. *The Christian Husband.* Vine Books, 1999.

Leman, Kevin. *Sex Begins in the Kitchen.* Fleming Revell, new edition, 1999.

Penner, Clifford, and Joyce Penner. *The Gift of Sex.* Word Publishing, 1981.

———. *Getting Your Sex Life Off to a Great Start.* Word Publishing, 1997.

Rainey, Dennis. *Simply Romantic Nights.* Family Life Publishing, 2001.

Rainey, Dennis, and Barbara Rainey. *Building Your Mate's Self-Esteem.* Thomas Nelson, 1995.

Roizen, Michael, M.D. *Real Age: Are You As Young As You Can Be?* HarperCollins, 1999.

Wheat, Ed. *Intended for Pleasure.* Fleming Revell, 1987.

12-26-03